Lost and Found

Lost and Found

Surviving Displacement, Finding Love, Uncovering Secrets

a memoir

Ann Avram Huber

Mishpucha
BOOKS

from our family to yours

In Memory of
My Grandmother, **Sara Marcus**
My Mother, **Netty Gleizer**
My Mother-in-Law, **Pesche Huber**

ISBN: 978-0-9883544-6-3
Library of Congress Control Number: 2017905741

Interior Design by Adept Content Solutions
Cover Design by Meg Souza

Mishpucha BOOKS

from our family to yours

Published by Mishpucha Books
Madison, NJ 07940
www.Mishpuchabooks.com

CONTENTS

Herm (exasperated):
"Where were you when God was
giving out patience?"

Ann (feisty):
"I was in the intelligence line
for the second time!"

Ann to Herm:
"Sometimes I love you so much
I think my heart will burst."

PREFACE

MADELINE ALBRIGHT and I share a similar history. I too was born abroad, left Europe as a child, became a lawyer, and got involved in politics. Like her, I learned only late in life that significant truths about my heritage and, indeed, who I was, had been kept from me. Why did I not become Secretary of State? To what extent was it talent or luck or the result of some other forces? To what extent was my path shaped by other people's choices or mine? Or the tumultuous forces of history? Or was it fate?

> *Destiny is no matter of chance. It is a matter of choice.*
> *It is not a thing to be waited for, it is a thing to be achieved.*
>
> William Jennings Bryan

Chapter One

GALATI

AS A CHILD, I often tried to imagine my parents' wedding day. My mother did not want to discuss her wedding and it wouldn't have occurred to me to ask my father. We never talked about the past. My fantasies drew heavily on what I'd seen in romantic movies like "South Pacific," because I had so few facts to go on. The only clues were the few worn, professional wedding photos among the family pictures kept in a shoebox. Perhaps I spent so much time with this box of old sepia photos because, apart from a china doll and a jar of buttons, it was the only thing I had to play with. I spent hours in our tiny apartment in Haifa, Israel, sorting, studying, and labeling the wedding pictures. Somehow, perhaps because of the way my mother brushed off the subject, I sensed a mystery. I was hungry for more information.

In those photos, my mother Netty wore a magnificent, long-sleeved gown. A veil descended from a headdress into a long train and she carried a large bouquet of flowers. "They were white," was all my mother was willing to say. My father Sandu was dressed in a fashionable, immaculately tailored suit with a white bow tie, white gloves and black top hat. They made a lovely couple, elegant,

Netty and Sandu's Wedding, 1939.

beautiful—and so young! Netty was 16, Sandu 24. It was 1939 in Galati, Romania, three months before Germany attacked Poland, launching World War II. The carefree, innocent faces I saw in those photos would soon be lined with worry.

My mother was born in 1923 in Galati, (pronounced "Galatz"), a large seaport about 150 miles east of Bucharest on the banks of the Danube River. She was named after her paternal grandmother, as were four of her cousins, according to the Jewish custom of naming children after deceased kin. The family kept the cousins straight with nicknames—Netty the Eldest, Netty the Shortest, Netty the Redhead. I was never certain of my mother's nickname, but I think it would translate as something like Netty the Cunning. This made sense to me:

she was smart, and a survivor who navigated through a difficult and complicated life. In her later years, when I devoted a great deal of time to her care, she should have been called Netty the Cranky. If I arrived late because I was tending to my children or grandchildren, she was always unhappy. She was expert at sucking the joy out of seeing her. "Annie, they're taking advantage of you. You spoil them too much." One of my grandchildren nicknamed her Great Netty, perhaps an ironic name, or perhaps simply a contraction of Great Grandma Netty. Unfortunately for both of us, I remained the center of Netty's life well into my adulthood. She insisted she did not need friends and relied exclusively on me. Yet, until she was so old she began to fear her own death, she revealed precious little about herself: she held her emotions in check and her full story a mystery.

In the first decades of the 20th century, Galati was a thriving seaport with a population of about 100,000, including 20,000 Jews whose ancestors could be traced back to the 16th century. Galati had survived successive occupations, beginning with the Romans and later by the Turks of the Ottoman Empire. During the Ottoman occupation of the nineteenth century mob attacks against Jews were not uncommon in which Jews were either killed on the spot or driven into the Danube to drown.

By the time of my mother's birth, anti-Semitism was less prevalent than during the Ottoman rule, though always lurking. After World War I, Galati became the center of Romanian Zionism. When my mother was a young child, Galati had 22 synagogues.

Films documenting life in Galati around 1944 show tram tracks, but it seems most things were moved by horse and wagon or by women balancing large woven baskets on poles across their shoulders. Yet, my mother boasted to me that Galati had a beautiful railroad station with daily service to Bucharest. She always said the stone building with slate tiles at the Madison, New Jersey train station reminded her of Galati. A picture of Galati's old train station circa

1890 shows an appealing stone building with pitched slate roof. It could have been transplanted from a quaint Swiss village and built to survive forever. When my mother talked about Galati's trains, I did not yet have any notion of the role they had played in her life.

My grandfather putting on "tefillin;" Mamaia, 1953.

My grandparents settled in Galati shortly after they were married. My grandfather, Carol Marcus, born in 1897 in the nearby village of Tecuci, and my grandmother, Sara, born in 1901 in the village of Podu Turkului, were first cousins who married around 1920. It was not uncommon among that culture at that time for cousins to marry including first cousins.

Although he was already quite old when I was born, I remember my grandfather well, as a gentle, kind, soft-spoken man who loved to laugh. Each morning until he passed away when I was six, I observed him begin the ritual of morning prayers by wrapping the small leather boxes called phylacteries (containing prayers from the Torah) around his arm, hand, and fingers and on his forehead. Short and portly, he resembled my grandmother, the family matriarch whom we called Mamaia, a childish contraction of the Romanian counterpart of "Big Momma" which my cousin Mircea, the first grandchild, could not manage to pronounce. My grandfather became Tataia.

Netty (left) and her sister Lontzi, late 1920s.

Mamaia carried on the traditions in the home, lighting Shabbat candles every Friday night and decorating the house with tree branches for Sukkot, the Jewish celebration of the harvest.

Having lost their son, Isaac, before he reached the age of one, Carol and Sara doted on my mother and her younger sister, Lontzi. In a framed photograph my mother kept prominently on the wall near her bed until her death, she and Lontzi, then five and two years old, are sitting on a stone railing. They have matching short haircuts, the hair curling up from pearl stud earrings to full bangs topped with big fabric bows, and wear similar outfits. My mother is wearing a dark velvet dress with a round lace collar, her feet politely crossed at the ankles showing off freshly polished white shoes. Lontzi has on a print dress with the same round lace collar, a long string of white pearls and black patent shoes. While my mother holds a small purse, Lontzi is holding a child-size umbrella on her lap that stylishly matches her dress. Neither child is smiling. My mother looks worried. Lontzi's light eyes are piercing and determined. "Lontzi would not sit still for the photographer," my mother told me. "She was jealous that I was holding a little purse; so she was given a string of pearls to wear because she was crying. Lontzi always got her way."

Netty in secondary school.

My mother was a bright, pretty child who developed early into a beautiful woman. She was pale skinned, like the china doll I played with as a child, and had dark wavy hair, a round face with a small nose and full lips. I inherited her hazel eyes and her smooth silky skin, but otherwise I thought I more resembled my father. I even had his widow's peak. Scouring my parents' photographs, I found one of Netty in her teens, a studious girl wearing a beret who bore a stunning resemblance to the serious girl in my own third-grade school photo.

Like most other girls from well-to-do Jewish families in Romania, my mother was given a liberal arts education. She studied French and English, mathematics, embroidery, and needlework. I still have some pieces of beautifully embroidered linen tablecloths, towels and wall hangings she prepared for her own trousseau before her marriage. Although proud of her ability to do computations in her head, she never studied any kind of science and was always terrified of insects. While she could read, write and speak Romanian, English, and French, my mother always worked as a saleslady. Lontzi, on the other hand, who studied business administration and was also good at computation, never worked outside the home. All my life, Netty and Lontzi lived continents apart. On the rare occasions when I saw them together, my mother would lament the irony of their education. "Lontzi, you were the one who was supposed to go out to work and I was supposed to stay home," she accused. My mother often spoke in accusations.

My father, Sandu Avram, was born in 1915 in Bacau, at the foot of the Carpathian Mountains in the Moldova region of Romania, where the surname "Avram" was recorded as far back as 1772. His mother died giving birth to her fifth child, Lily, when Sandu was seven years old. I was given her Hebrew name of Hanna. Sandu never spoke about his childhood, but according to my mother, his father remarried a young, selfish woman who didn't want anyone else's children. Lily, Sandu and their other siblings were eventually separated, and sent to live with different relatives. Somehow, Lily and my father maintained a remarkably close bond. I never met any of the other siblings, though I once found a picture of a strange family that I thought might include my mysterious aunts and uncles. My mother explained that the only relative in the photo was a brother of Sandu's who had made his way to Israel with his wife and children after the War. "We lost touch with them after a short time," she said. Apart from this brother, Sandu and Lily were the only members of the family to survive the Holocaust.

One of Sandu's brothers who made his way to Israel
before/after the Second World War.

While Lily was sent to live with an elderly couple on a farm, Sandu went to Galati to stay with an uncle who ran a gambling hall, where Sandu worked in exchange for his room and board. My father never learned to read or write, but he was intelligent, and I think, courageous as he tried to make his way in a strange city despite his painful shyness. Though he had no marketable skills, he was young, strong, and extremely handsome with very dark eyes and dark curly hair that cascaded back in waves from a widow's peak. He was a dead ringer for Clark Gable in my favorite movie, *Gone with the Wind*. But the resemblance was superficial. The gambling hall never suited Sandu, who was always shy, quiet and hardly a risk taker.

Sandu in Israel.

I believe, however, that when 17-year-old Sandu met my grandfather, Carol Marcus, in Galati, he saw hope and opportunity, and followed through on developing a relationship. Carol might have seen a reflection of his own shy, charming smile in Sandu's broad smile and frequent blush, and almost certainly responded to his intelligence, street smarts, and willingness to learn. Carol decided to take the young man under his wing. My grandfather had by then become a well-to-do member of the Jewish community, and owned a shoe store called the Cocusul de Argint (Silver Rooster). He taught Sandu the shoe business, brought him to his home for family meals and even arranged for him to have a bar mitzvah since Sandu's family had taken no interest in the boy's education, religious or otherwise.

My grandfather's store in Galati on the corner of Tecuci and General Berthelot (streets no longer exist). My grandfather, Carol Marcus, in doorway, Netty in front of him, Sandu second from right.

Over the next seven years, Sandu became a loyal part of the Marcus family. Their connection is evident in a 1931 snapshot that depicts Sandu, then seventeen years old, standing to one side of the main entrance of the store in a suit and tie with hands by his side, and his head held up proudly, looking very satisfied to be there. My grandfather, also in a suit and tie stands in the main entrance, potbelly jutting out—potbellies run in the family. My mother, then nine years old, is in the picture as well, with her hands at her hips and her head cocked to one side with a sly smile. They're all standing below a regal sign bearing my grandfather's name, Carol Marcus. I have often wondered, what were they thinking? They were so young.

Sandu was always deferential to both Carol and Sara as if they'd been his own parents, and as Netty grew into a young beauty, he fell deeply in love with her; when she was sixteen, he asked Carol for his daughter's hand in marriage. It was no great surprise that Carol consented. Marriage into the family provided status, acceptance, and financial security—much sought after by Sandu and willingly shared by Carol. Both my grandfather and father were engaged in the

general culture and the vibrant Jewish community—a community
that maintained the high school from which my mother graduated,
and also created institutions such as a hospital, aid for the poor, and
orphanages which served Jews and Christians alike with the financial
support of the Romanian authorities.

I can still picture my father, leaning on one knee as he assisted a
client who was trying on shoes, as I saw him do thirty years later. He
taught me to appreciate a shapely, leather shoe. He loved a stylish shoe
and would hold it up on one hand like a treasure, supporting it with
the other hand from below. Whenever we bought new shoes, he would
examine them to offer his stamp of approval.

My mother was 24 when she and Sandu left Galati, but she always
spoke of it proudly and fondly, forever remaining loyal to the city of
her birth. By then, she, my father, and my grandparents were already
waiting with hundreds of thousands of other Romanian Jews for visas
to Palestine. They all wanted to escape a repeat of the Holocaust and
the tyranny of the Russians who had supplanted the Germans as World
War II ended.

Chapter Two

HAIFA

THREE MONTHS before Germany attacked Poland in September 1939,
Netty and Sandu married. Soon my father was conscripted into the
Romanian Army. Due to his affiliation with my mother's family, he
could afford a fine uniform and his own horse. A surviving military
portrait showed my father looking very distinguished in his uniform.
The Romanian army looked very good in their uniforms but was
defeated quite quickly.

Romania, which traditionally considered itself more aligned with
France than with its geographic neighbors, tried to remain neutral
before World War II. However, by 1940, Romania's King Carol II
had no alternative but to abdicate to ultra-right forces, led by Ion
Antonescu. Antonescu was a pro-Nazi politician who passed numerous
anti-Semitic laws such as those defining who is a Jew; laws requiring
mass firing of Jews from various positions; government supported
massacres, looting, pillaging and pogroms in Bucharest, Iasi and other
substantial population centers. The Jews suffered terrible atrocities, but
he was not interested in mass deportations to German concentration
camps. Romania joined the Axis nations of Germany, Italy, and Japan.

13

Sandu in his military uniform, 1939.

In Romania alone, 270,000 Jewish souls died during the holocaust. As World War II ended, an Iron Curtain descended across Europe separating Russia (then known as the Union of Soviet Socialist Republics or USSR) and its occupied territories including Romania and Poland from Western Europe. Millions of Jewish people, who had survived Nazi persecution only to find themselves behind the Iron Curtain, were desperate to leave. Most wanted to go to Israel. Yet, the USSR was loath to let anyone leave. A reduced population was inconsistent with its plans for world domination.

My parents and grandparents applied for a visa to Palestine as soon as there was a governmental agency ready to take the application, sometime around 1946. The United Nations had finally voted to recognize the creation of an independent State of Israel in 1948. I was born in 1950. Nine months later my parents were granted permission to leave for Israel. My grandparents followed shortly thereafter, arriving in Israel in 1951. When we left, we were required to relinquish our Romanian citizenship, our personal possessions and even our personal legal documents, such as birth and marriage certificates. A simple passport named all three of us. It was the only proof I had of my relationship to my parents.

Our ship brought us to Haifa, an industrial port on the slopes of Mount Carmel where it met the Mediterranean Sea. Although Haifa has historically been a center of industry, it was also the site of two universities and home to the Baha'i Temple's world-renowned gold dome and gardens. From any hillside one could always see the sun shimmering from the sea to the golden dome.

Outsmarting the Romanian authorities as other wealthier Jews had, my parents smuggled out money by sewing a few gold coins into the hems of their clothing. However, much of the other precious jewelry and gold, which my parents entrusted to a messenger, was stolen by him. Many years later they found out the "Devil" was living in Sao Paulo, Brazil—too late to recover anything or even prove any transaction had even taken place.

My parents with me (9 mos) in Bucharest before we left Romania.

Too proud to take government assistance in Haifa, or maybe too much of a snob, my father refused to accept public housing in one of the new and hastily built outlying settlements where many of my mother's relatives settled. Instead, he found an apartment in Haifa, a bus ride away from my mother's favorite cousin, Shelley. Shelley had made her way to Israel in the wave of young Zionists who left Europe in the 1930s. An ardent Zionist, Shelley had a government job for her entire adult life. She and her family always lived in public housing. Her daughters, Tzila and Tova were my constant childhood companions. I have vivid memories of holding on to the railing on the bus as it often sped down and around the hill just in time for their stop.

My grandparents soon joined us and we shared a terribly small space for five people—just two rooms. My parents and I slept in a multi-purpose room while my grandparents slept in the kitchen, another small and narrow space where they unfolded a bed every night. We shared a bathroom with another family. Their doorway opened to a shared courtyard, too, but I have no memory of them. One way to achieve privacy is just to pretend no one else is there.

My birthday party at 8 years old. Mamaia far right,
Netty third from right. I'm fourth from the right.

An armoire and dining table dominated our main space where we celebrated my fifth birthday with cake, candles and school friends, including my best friend, Anda. Our only window looked out onto the shared courtyard, laid with large slabs of marble, everything the color of chalk as it baked in the sun. Every week, a young Arab woman sitting crossed-legged, washed our clothes and sheets in an old tub, wringing them out by hand, and hanging them across the courtyard to dry. It was also in the courtyard that I chased, and was chased, by the three young boys who lived next door. I have warm, sentimental memories of their mother who taught me how to embroider. I still cherish a small Torah scroll replica on the cover of which I embroidered a flower.

One of my other earliest childhood memories starts on my parents' bed, tucked into the corner of the main room, under the large window, the sun shining in. In my sixth year, I got the mumps, the pain of which could only be soothed by cold compresses on my lumpy little neck. I lay in bed, day after day, staring at an uneven pattern of tape crisscrossing the window. It was taped, as many windows were, to prevent it from shattering should a bomb land on our section of Haifa during the 1956 Arab-Israeli war.

I understood little of why Israel had invaded Egypt, though my parents often talked to me about our safety being threatened by the surrounding Arab nations. I was worried about the possibility of war, but I was never actually afraid. At that time, it seemed that we feared Egypt most because it was the strongest of the nations. Every one talked about Nasser, then President of Egypt. War became inevitable after Egypt nationalized the Suez Canal, cutting off Israeli shipping from the Gulf of Suez. My recovery took as long as the war, less than a week, since Israel agreed to a cease fire after the United Nations assured Israel's access to the Indian Ocean through the Gulf of Aqaba. No bombs were dropped in Haifa.

In a neighborhood near Shelley's apartment, my father opened a small grocery store. There was not much need for shoe stores then in Haifa; few immigrants had the money for such luxuries. The store was next door to an Arab café—in 1951, many Jews and Arabs lived side by side in Haifa in relative harmony. Despite the flight of a large portion of the Arab population after the establishment of the Israeli state, there remained in Israel some Arab tribes friendly to the Jews. They lived and worked among us and even served in the Israeli army.

My parents both worked all day while the Arabic music and the smell of strong Turkish coffee wafted into the store. Outside the café were a few small, low tables where Arab men sat enjoying their coffee and smoking at all hours of the day.

My mother, who never cooked, learned to pickle cabbage, cucumbers and tomatoes in large, wooden barrels, which were displayed in front of the store. If I close my eyes, I can still smell the sour pickles and fragrant Turkish coffee blended together with all the other food smells like onions and garlic. There, in that little store, they labored six days a week. Shabbat was sacred. After all, it was a national holiday.

It was left to my grandparents, mostly my grandmother, to take care of me. Mamaia was petite, with short gray hair and lively hazel eyes. She had suffered from diabetes since the age of twenty, requiring daily insulin injections that she administered herself. Nonetheless, she was the matriarch of the family in the full sense of the word. My father always deferred to her and came to consider her as his mother. He spoke to her very respectfully, always using formal Romanian speech and his best manners in her presence.

My mother was thoroughly dependent on her. Both she and my father granted her full authority. Since Mamaia took care of me,

My mother, Mamaia, and me, 1958.

Little Red Riding Hood costume, 1954.

did the cooking, sewing and knitting and pretty much managed the household, my mother did whatever my grandmother told her to do. Mamaia always had knitting needles or sewing in her hands. Every year, she made an elaborate costume for me for the Purim holiday. In various years, I was Little Red Riding Hood, a Chinese man, a ballerina, and even a Scotsman in a kilt with a tassel on each of my socks. No detail was overlooked.

I spent time with my parents on Shabbat. They were polar opposites. My mother was the practical one who was anxious about everything. I believe she felt loving and supportive of me, yet she was conflicted about showing it. There was nothing she would not do for me if she thought it was necessary; however, for some reason she worried about spoiling me, and withheld anything she considered unnecessary. When I was older, I was given an allowance. I used it to buy 5 cents worth of candy after school and to go to the movies. If I wanted to buy her a birthday present or a mother's day gift, I had to borrow the money from her and repay it with my allowance. At some point, that didn't feel right. It felt like unnecessary deprivation, which I never imposed on my own children.

Sandu, for his part, was a generous gift-giver, a romantic who preferred not to deal or could not deal with his inability to earn an adequate living. As a rare treat, my father would bring for me a single yellow Delicious apple. He would hold it up, perched on his fingertips and playfully proclaim, "It has red cheeks just like you."

In preparation for Shabbat, every Friday, Mamaia and I walked to the outdoor market to purchase the ingredients for our Friday night family dinner. Walking down to the market on Herzl Street, my grandmother would test my math skills, preparing me for the day when I would have to drive a hard bargain with the food vendors myself. In Romanian she would ask, "How much does two times two make? How much is twelve plus four? How much is forty-five divided by nine?" I always answered in Hebrew. The math drills were beneficial, but outweighed by the heavy watermelon I carried uphill on the way back. A mule-drawn carriage delivered milk and the children all ran out to watch the milkman dole out a potful at a time.

We had a set menu every Friday night—roasted chicken, rice, peppers and watermelon. Mamaia also baked a cake, a variation of a pound cake, in a "Wundertopf"—Yiddish for an Israeli invention for baking on top of a kerosene burner rather than an oven. It looked like a covered Bundt pan, slightly modified, with a center hole which fit between the flame and the pot. I had my own toy-size one. My small cake pan baked atop the Wundertopf.

My parents always came home in time for our weekly feast. After they bathed, Mamaia and my mother lit Shabbat candles and our little family sat at our dining table. Following the main meal, I cut my little cake into tiny, one inch slices for everyone to share. I was clearly a contributing family member.

There were other rituals on Shabbat, and not the religious kind.
In the morning, I would accompany my father, dolled up in my
Shabbat dress, to meet his buddies in the local park. While the men
sat and talked about history and politics, I ran around and played.
Every Saturday afternoon, the adults took a well-deserved nap. In
the evening, my parents went to the movies and took me along.
Unfortunately, one movie, "The Inn of the Sixth Happiness" with
Ingrid Bergman, was responsible for a recurring nightmare that
survived well into my adulthood. A scene in the movie still sends
shivers down my spine though I have not dared to see it since: bare-
chested men are dancing with colorfully dressed women who are
beheaded with enormous, curved, sharp-looking knives.

After I started school, I took the short walk every day to the
Alliance School on Herzl Street, walking back home to play with the
neighbors' children. On special days, I was allowed to play with Anda
even though she lived in a better neighborhood and was given piano
lessons. In a small sepia photograph, taken in our courtyard, Anda, with
short curly dark hair and I, also with short but auburn hair, displayed
our birthday dresses. We crowed proudly, "Aren't these beautiful?" as
we twirled and modeled them for the camera in various poses.

In 1958, me (left) and best friend, Anda.

At the conclusion of World War II, the Jewish Agency for Israel asked for reparations, restitution, and indemnification for the victims of the Holocaust. Not until 1953 did West Germany agree to pay $845 million to the State of Israel over the next 14 years. It was to be paid partly in credit for oil and partly with various steel, agricultural, and industrial equipment including tens of thousands of Volkswagen "beetles."

Until some of the reparations made their way into the economy, which did not happen for many years, life in the young State of Israel was difficult, conditions were harsh. There was not enough food, not enough housing, not enough jobs for the hundreds of thousands of immigrants who made their way there after the war. Not so for me. I was happy and secure, barefoot much of the time, always free to run out the door to play. By the age of ten, Israel's pioneer spirit had already left its imprint on me. Many Americans have adopted the Israeli word for it—"chutzpah." My husband calls me "feisty." Others say I am a fighter who does not give up easily.

Chapter Three

MONTREAL

WITHOUT WARNING, my parents announced we would be going to Canada to start again. As we sat on my bed, on the other side of the room I shared with them, opposite our only window, my mother explained, "We're moving far away, to a new place. It will be cold there and there will be snow just like in Romania. There you will meet your aunt and cousin but Mamaia will not be coming with us." Haifa was my home. I was attached to my friends, my grandparents, my school, my street, even my little bed. I was bewildered.

"You cannot tell any of your friends that you are leaving, not even Anda. But, don't worry; you can come back anytime." Of course, I believed her. I was only 9 years old. To ease my distress, my mother showed me a new gray wool coat trimmed with a fur collar and gray boots with a matching lining. My eyes widened at this rare gift. "I prepared these especially for you," she said, as I examined the strange new clothes.

"What about Mamaia?"

"Mamaia will come later." I believed her.

No one explained why we had to leave Israel, nor exactly where Canada was. A fourth grader, I had no concept of a world greater than Israel and her neighbors. I thought it would be just a bus ride back from Canada, just like the bus ride we took visiting relatives in Tsvat Israel's northern mountains.

Nor did I understand why I had to keep it a secret, but I was young enough not to question and old enough to obey. I sensed that we were in some kind of trouble. Something was very wrong.

Only a few days after my mother told me we were leaving, long after I had fallen asleep, I was awakened for our journey. My mother's cousin Chaim, Shelley's brother, came to transport us to the airport in the ubiquitous Volkswagen beetle taxi.

In the dark, I climbed out of the taxi onto the tarmac, up a ladder, and boarded a plane. It was like a scene out of Casablanca—dead of night, a warm wind howling, engines roaring, gasoline smell polluting the air, quickly being shepherded onto the plane as I clutched a new sweater from Mamaia. I never got to say goodbye to either my cousins or my friends. For years, I felt the clandestine departure with a heavy heart.

We expected to fly directly to Montreal, but an early snowstorm required a stop in Labrador, Newfoundland. It was a gray wasteland with nothing to see. I had always had a problem with motion sickness, which had been unexpectedly exacerbated by my first experience with beef aboard the airplane. Or, maybe it was fear of the unknown that had unsettled me. Another takeoff and landing only made me sick a second time during that trip.

Montreal, in Quebec Province, Canada, is an island in the St. Lawrence River first discovered by French explorer Jacques Cartier, seeking a northwest route to Asia in 1535. The French influence persists although the English conquered the City in 1760, resulting in tremendous industry, growth and wealth by and for the English. When we arrived in 1959, French-speaking Quebecois were an oppressed minority for whom the Separatist Movement had yet to gain prominence. We knew little of this conflict when we arrived. What we knew was that there was a large Jewish community and a Canadian population that welcomed its immigrants.

In Montreal's Dorval airport, we landed on top of a thin layer of snow, the first of the winter and the first I'd ever seen. My mother was giddy when she saw the snow which reminded her of Romania. "Aren't the snowflakes soft and wet? Stick out you tongue," she told me as she demonstrated. "See how they float down onto your hair and face?" I did not know what to make of the cold white specks of water on my skin and tongue. We'd left behind a warm howling wind and faced a very cold one instead.

We were greeted by friendly immigration officials who smiled and seemed genuinely happy to see us. Late that night, after we made our way through immigration and customs, where I did not understand a single word, I immediately recognized my father's sister, Aunt Lily, who came to meet us. Lily and Sandu looked so much alike—dark skin, dark curly hair, widow's peak, dark brown eyes and the same shy smile—it was uncanny. Lily was shy, even more shy than my father, and she tilted her head down a little toward her chest as she greeted us. She was very tall and bent down to grab my arms to hold me at arms-length so she could look me over before kissing me. Her skin felt so rough on my face, unlike my mother's soft cheek.

They drove us to the apartment they shared with their daughter, Anna, on Linton Street in a relatively new neighborhood. The streets were divided by a grassy median planted with young trees and lined with neatly laid out, small lawns alongside the sidewalks. Many such neighborhoods sprang up in the 1950s, and look much the same today although the trees now tower over the medians.

The neatly furnished apartment was on the third floor of a walk up, with multiple bedrooms and a balcony overlooking the street. I was not surprised to find that Lily shared my mother's compulsion for cleanliness. My parents and I shared a room with a Singer sewing machine with a manual pedal just like the one on which Mamaia had sewn my yearly Purim costumes. "Who would sew the next one?" I asked myself.

Lily had met her husband Julius (nicknamed Lulu) in Romania when he was on his way back to his native Austria from Russia, where he had ended up after a forced march as prisoner of the Nazis. They'd last seen Sandu and Netty when they came to visit in Galati during the War. My mother told me, "I gave Lily a negligee as a wedding gift. It was a used one that Mamaia and I altered for her. There was nothing else in wartime." Lily and Lulu left Galati for Austria, where they were imprisoned in a labor camp. After the fall of the Nazi regime, they spent some time in an Austrian displaced-persons camp before immigrating to Montreal in 1951, about the same time we were making our way to Israel.

Over the years, Lily and my father's correspondence had been rare since my father did not know how to read or write. Though there was a palpable closeness between them, having grown up separately, Sandu and Lily did not know how to relate to each other. After a fifteen-year separation, they barely looked at each other. They avoided direct eye contact and they hardly spoke. They were both not only extremely shy, but also socially awkward in general not to mention a bit paranoid.

Our stay with Lily ended abruptly because of an unfortunate misunderstanding. Due to space constraints, my aunt stored a bag of oranges in one of the bedrooms. Sandu thought she was hiding food from us, an unforgivable insult. This resulted in a terrible argument, lots of screaming and accusations between these two fragile and insecure beings.

That evening, to assert his independence and his pride, my father took my mother and me out to dinner at the counter of a local pharmacy—my first restaurant dining experience and novel food. We ate grilled cheese sandwiches and French fries with gravy, a Canadian specialty called "poutine." No one seemed to care that it wasn't kosher. The meal was just slightly better than the counter food at Woolworth's five and dime store where I would have many future meals.

Our first home in Montreal was a modest, one-bedroom basement apartment (which we shared with a colony of silverfish) on Decelles Street, about three blocks from Lily's. Decelles was a steep grade down the west side of Mount Royal, two blocks from the University of Montreal and one block from the drugstore where we had our first "restaurant" meal. With the apartment windows at street level, at first it seemed like an improvement over the below street level window in

Haifa. Alas, it was not. In Haifa, the window was still up from ground level and I could not touch the grass outside the window.

The apartment was furnished with donations my mother and I picked up at the B'nai B'rith thrift store and carried home on the bus, plus the goodies my father rescued from the trash collection area in the bowels of the building. One great find was an entire collection of 78-RPM records of wonderful music by artists such as Mario Lanza. I can still hear the scratchy version of *O Sole Mio* which I listened to over and over. With few friends, I had a lot of time to listen to the many classical records like Beethoven's *Ninth Symphony* and Mozart's *Messiah*. The record player too was a hand-me-down, as was the little black and white television set, given to us by a kindly, better-off neighbor. She must have given us a lot of things because I still remember the short, large-breasted and portly woman with dark hair and a booming voice who came to deliver treasures.

The worst hand-me-down, origin unknown, was a folding bed on which I slept in the living room. I hated that bed and lived in fear of its collapse. Many nights, the top half did just that in the middle of the night, waking me without warning and flinging my head down backwards where silverfish, the scourge of all basements (though certainly better than cockroaches), threatened my existence. I asked my mother, "Can't we take a bus back to Haifa?"

On our first day in Montreal, my mother and I walked three blocks from Lily's apartment to Young Israel, a private parochial school. I don't know if she was unaware of the high cost, or she was willing to pay whatever it took, but when she tried to enroll me, fortunately for all of us, the principal turned me down because I spoke too much Hebrew but neither English nor French. Instead, he suggested I attend a public school for a short time to learn English. That was the last they saw either of us.

My mother and I walked two blocks to the Logan School on Darlington Avenue. There were both Protestant and Catholic public schools. In the former, the dominant language was English, although French was also taught. The reverse was true in the Catholic schools. The Logan School was Protestant. We entered through the front door of the sprawling one story building. The principal tested my cognitive abilities by pointing to numbers on a calendar that he expected me to read off in English. I could not. He placed me in the "slow learners" class—always the "dummy" class to me.

I was led to a classroom and shown to a seat. I know I was introduced because I heard my name, but I understood nothing else. I do remember copying the date, December 1, 1959, learning the cursive capital letter "D" following along as another student showed me how to form the letter. That day and many others, as a "slow learner," my teacher sent me to the back of the small classroom with another student, smarty-pants Allan. It was humiliating. Due to my conspicuous lack of "intelligence" I had to go over the Dick and Jane early readers with the catchphrase "Run Spot Run" countless times with Allan. It did not take long before I memorized those books, but I had little idea what the words meant.

My teacher, Mrs. Zinman, was cruel and unfeeling in other ways. The class recited the pledge of allegiance every morning, which of course, I did not know. I memorized those words phonetically, too, but they meant nothing to me. I pronounced many words incorrectly. She regularly humiliated me by calling me out, insisting I repeat words that I mispronounced. It was the worst year of my short life. With no one to talk to in school, I was miserable.

In retrospect, I find it very strange that my mother, who spoke both English and French, made no effort to teach me. Until now, we spoke both Hebrew and Romanian at home, though my father's Hebrew was sketchy at best. Now as I struggled in school, they both refused to speak to me in Hebrew, which only served to improve my now useless Romanian. My mother didn't start speaking to me in English until much later in life. Sandu and I spoke little—he was always somewhat detached from the everyday goings on at home—but it was always Romanian between us.

With the loss of my first language at home, and my inability to communicate at school, I felt there was no longer any safe place to be. Yet, my parents were so pleased with this Protestant school, attended primarily by Jewish immigrant children, that we never talked about the private school again and my religious education came to a halt.

Lucille Ball became my primary English teacher. I watched *I Love Lucy* for many years. At first, I thought her name was "Lucy O'Ball"— there were so many other English surnames starting with "O." But when neither school nor television resulted in my learning enough English to master the materials of fourth grade, my mother took the school's advice and engaged a tutor.

Hannah, a gentle teenager who reminded me of the teenager next door in Haifa was a joy compared to the torture of school. And she taught me a lot more than English. It was from Hannah that I began to learn how to fit into the culture. She curled my hair into a more fashionable style. She critiqued my outfits and helped me put together more stylish ones. Together, we listened to popular music like *Tossin' and Turnin'* by Bobby Lewis and Del Shannon's *Runaway*.

Still at school for some time, I remained a stranger in a strange land, didn't speak the language, wore hand-me-downs and knew no one except a cousin who pretended not to know me during recess, even for the couple of weeks that we lived in the same apartment. Yes, Lily's daughter Anna, who was only a year younger, and also an only child, went to the same school. But no one would have guessed we were first cousins. Why did she ignore me when I felt so alone? Was I a threat to her because her mother doted on me? I was Lily's only niece, and she showered me with love and attention.

"As a young child, I went to live on a farm with an elderly aunt and uncle. Even though I hardly knew Sandu, I always loved you because you were his child," Lily explained. She was affectionate, generous and protective of me. While there was no doubt that Lily was fierce in her protection of Anna as well and would have killed anyone who would try to harm her, as sometimes happens between mothers and daughters she did not show the same affection to Anna, always criticizing her and comparing her to others.

Anna and her father, on the other hand, were very close and even looked alike. Lulu, too, was always very kind to me but very quiet, often deferring to Lily to avoid conflict.

Lily, Lulu, and Anna soon moved away from the neighborhood to the suburb of Cote St. Luc (nicknamed "Cote St. Jew"), so my embarrassment on the playground was short-lived. After they moved, we rarely saw them but my aunt always remembered my birthdays with presents—a child-size beautifully dressed doll, a ring with my birthstone, a green party dress.

Anna and I did not get to play much, but despite that and the rough start, we eventually bonded. As we got older, we got to know each other better, realized that we had much in common and a powerful affinity pulled us together. Eventually, my childhood resentment melted away. We have felt close as adults, each of us growing up lonely, only children with parents damaged by war and displacement.

Chapter Four

Becoming Canadian, Eh?

My folding bed was set up nightly in front of an old, upright piano that finally enabled me to take lessons. In Israel, my interest in piano lessons had been diverted by a flirtation with a recorder, but my wish finally came true in Montreal. My mother arranged for lessons offered by the school, where we were taught on a cardboard keyboard set up on a desk. My teacher was a fellow immigrant from Hungary, Mr. Andre, who later gave me private lessons until I graduated from high school at age seventeen. He was a quiet, soft-spoken man with the longest, slimmest, strongest fingers I ever saw dance across the keys. Under his tutelage, I continued with the Toronto Conservatory of Music yearly exams, graduating from their program at the end of high school. Mr. Andre promised to play at my wedding.

With Lily's help, my father quickly found work in the negligee factory where she worked. The factory was not far from our neighborhood and my father walked there daily, but he complained about it bitterly and incessantly.

Eleven years old, playing the piano.

My mother got a job in a small, privately owned grocery store on St. Lawrence Street, Montreal's long-established equivalent to New York's Delancey Street, both neighborhoods populated by successive waves of immigrants. In the early 1960s, all the shops on bustling St. Lawrence Street were operated by Jewish immigrants and frequented by the newest arrivals. Moishe's and Schwartz's Steakhouses are still present reminders of that time. Often, the noise was deafening especially when the street hawkers worked their way up and down the street with used clothing, pots, pickles—you name it.

My mother worked in the tiny, smelly grocery store through the worst months of our first winter. It was a difficult environment, with no heat in the brutal Montreal winter and my mother's hands were raw, chapped and bleeding from reaching into the waist-high wooden pickle barrel to fill customer orders. Unlike my father, my mother never complained about her job, at least not to me, working stoically, determined to make a life for me. I see this now as evidence of how she had toughened up as a result of the multiple migrations. She had come a long way from the embroidering days of Galati.

I realize now how remarkably resourceful she became, although some today might call it stingy. She turned every sack of flour into an apron or towel, every napkin was cut in half to make two, and she always went shopping with a list and sales coupons, never buying anything not on her list. Her cupboards and refrigerator had nothing extra beyond the week's meals. She did not pass that characteristic onto me.

In what I admired even then as a remarkable example of her frugality, each year she wore a new hat for Rosh Hashanah (Jewish New Year). Of course, she did not buy a new hat each year. Rather, she exchanged the previous year's hat for a new one at Eaton's Department Store. Each receipt had the date of the transaction, but without the year stamped on it. No wonder Eaton's went bankrupt after 130 years in business.

On one of my mother's first days off in the winter of 1960, she took me to see the movie, *Ben-Hur*, an epic with Charlton Heston about a Jewish prince, betrayed and sent into slavery by a Roman friend, who regains his freedom and comes back for revenge. The movie was in French with English subtitles that made very little difference to me since I couldn't understand or read either language. I did understand the dramatic, close up chariot scene, in which protruding blades from one chariot's wheel-spokes, methodically and brutally, sliced through the spokes of the wheels of the others. This scene only re-fueled my recurring nightmare of the Chinese dancers and still makes my heart race whenever I see a replay.

The violence in *Ben-Hur* was overwhelming for me, which might explain my life-long abhorrence of it. Who could have guessed Charlton Heston would become a spokesman for the NRA, an organization not exactly dedicated to promoting non-violence.

My father didn't work on Saturdays. During our first year in Montreal, he took care of me when my mother worked or whenever there was no program for me at the Neighborhood House on St. Lawrence Street. Since Sandu had no circle of friends as he'd had in Haifa, on Saturday mornings we either sat alone in nearby Kent Park or we ambled our way through Montreal's streets. Mostly, as we sat or walked we talked about history, government and politics, which ignited a life-long interest in these subjects for me.

"Do you remember who Ben-Gurion is?" he said one time.

"I remember he is the President of Israel."

"But, do you know how he got to be president?" he asked. "Let me tell you...."

When we got far from home, my father would have to coax me back. I was too tired to walk. He couldn't get on a city bus because he was fearful whenever confronted with anything unfamiliar. To him, a bus was a monstrous and uncontrollable machine. He never learned to drive for the same reason.

It became my responsibility to serve the meals my mother had prepared when she was at work. When she needed gallbladder surgery and was hospitalized for about a week, I was pleased that at age eleven I was able to cook for my father, if you could call what I did cooking. Mostly, I again served meals my mother had prepared in advance.

Years later, my father who remained painfully shy, tried to be sociable with my husband. Smiling awkwardly, he told Herm that I almost killed him when I tried to make gelatin by putting it in the freezer to congeal faster, where it froze without ever setting. It was like eating frozen crystals. My father was funny because as bad as it was he still tried to eat it all. I was pleased to hear him tell a story since he never really talked much to anyone but my mother, grandmother, and me.

I missed my grandmother who was still in Israel. However, I found some comfort and joy in our little family because this was the first and only time in my memory that we lived together without oversight from my grandparents.

Chapter Five

THERE IS NO GOING BACK

MY AUNT LONTZI and her family were finally granted visas to go
to Israel shortly after we left. According to my cousin, Rodica, when
she and her brother, Mircea, arrived in Haifa, she and Lontzi lived
with Mamaia in our old apartment. Rodica slept in the same bed I'd
slept in only a couple of years earlier. Lontzi's husband, Costel, lived
and worked elsewhere in Israel, in one of the new settlements, where
he tried unsuccessfully to establish a place for the family. Mircea, the
older of the cousins, lived on a kibbutz but was unhappy there. After
debating whether to join us in Canada, they moved to Brazil to join
friends from Romania. It was then, in 1962, that our grandmother
finally followed us to Montreal.

I learned years later from Rodica that my leaving Israel was just as
traumatic a separation for Mamaia as it was for me. She would not let
Rodica forget for a moment that she missed me terribly. "Nothing I
did was ever good enough or as good as you did," Rodica lamented to
me years later.

Rodica confided she had come to hate our grandmother for
the way she treated her. I was sad to hear of Mamaia's cruelty, but

I understood her desperate longing. Talking to Rodica about our grandmother seemed to bring us closer. Like me, she hated watching Mamaia go through her weekly buying frenzy at the food market. She felt bad for the food vendors.

By the time Mamaia was finally able to join us, I was a different person than the child she remembered. Mamaia noticed quickly that I had changed from a happy, carefree youngster into a not-so-happy 12-year-old, shaken to her core. Although I now had a real bed and my very own room in a new three-bedroom apartment on the third floor of a building with marble floors and stairs, I was miserable.

I still struggled to make it out of the dummy class and to form friendships with my peers. It was common for me stand conspicuously and painfully alone on the playground at recess. By then I understood that there would be no going back home for me. I realized I had to learn the foreign ways of a culture where Jews were the minority, and this did not come easily. Yes, I had learned to speak some English, to imitate others by repeating phrases, to read body language—not always correctly—and to infer missing pieces of information. I even learned how to cover up the gaps in my understanding or knowledge. It was not uncommon for me to get the wrong idea about what had been said and take offense, which would make me blush. My reaction was to swallow my pride rather than laugh along with the others.

I also did all the things that were expected of me like going to school, making superficial friends, helping the family navigate the difficult terrain. However, a part of me was missing, longing to return to Israel, where I felt I belonged. I didn't belong in Montreal. I felt the pain of my wound all the time, and I'm not sure it has ever fully healed. I still find that I get words mixed up—such as defuse and diffuse—and my mixed metaphors are the stuff of family lore.

I did not have very many friends in our first few years in Montreal, but for a little while I was part of a threesome. Esther who lived a block down the same street, Kathy who lived around the corner, and I were classmates. We walked to school together daily and were best of friends. Daily at lunch, we crossed the street to the small corner store to buy five cents worth of candy. More often, I saved my nickel for Saturday's morning matinees with them.

One day out of the blue, Esther shot me, verbally. She told me she was not allowed to play with me anymore. Her mother thought I was promiscuous. I didn't know the word but understood from her body language and speech what she meant. Apparently, unbeknownst to me, I was maturing faster than she was, which her mother saw as a threat to Esther. I was confused and heartbroken. I really liked Esther. She was witty, funny and pretty. Our friendship was so easy and comfortable. But we no longer spoke as we passed each other on the street or in school. Kathy, my one remaining friend, and I were friends through high school but Esther moved away about a year later and I never saw her again.

The adults around me showed little compassion, or understanding perhaps, for the trauma I suffered. Or perhaps they simply didn't understand my unhappiness although it was their role to be concerned about me. Perhaps it was just a generation more preoccupied with basic survival and their own traumas than with my emotional health. Unwittingly, the adults who loved me caused irreparable harm, shaking up my sense of security and self-confidence in part because of their continued false assurances that I could go back to the place where I felt safe. I was yanked from home to a stranger's land from which there was no quick departure or recovery. I felt lost.

For years, I yearned to go back, at least to visit or say a belated good-bye.

Chapter Six

RESILIENCY

THINGS STARTED TO IMPROVE when, a year or two later, a local shopping center was built only a block from my school, five blocks from our apartment. My mother applied for a sales job when Woolworth's sent out a hiring call. She landed a job because of her proficiency in both English and French although she mutilated English with such funny expressions as, "I beg your pardon me."

Every day after school I walked over to Woolworth's where I would spend the remainder of the afternoon, having milk and cookies at the old-fashioned luncheonette counter or chatting with my mother's friends. At the end of her shift, my mother and I would walk home together.

The other saleswomen (no men except for the manager) were like my foster parents, each with her own role in my life. Mary, an ugly spinster of Greek descent, with large protruding teeth, always smiled at me, watching, but saying little in her broken English. Sadly, she died young of a brain tumor. Madame La Robardier was childless and relied on my mother for advice about life. We spoke only French together which was a great help to me. Finally, there was Mrs. Klein, a Jewish grandmother to whom my mother went for advice and clothing. She lent my mother a dress to wear at my sweet sixteen and another for my wedding. It was also Mrs. Klein who gave me as a wedding present, a new copy of "Second Helpings," a now famous cookbook compiled by Montreal's B'nai B'rith Women from which I learned how to cook. My book was a first edition. One of my daughters has a thirteenth edition!

The other saleswomen at Woolworth's were friends as well as foster mothers. We consulted on my party dress for the sixth grade dance. A boy named George, a very nice and studious young man, had asked me to accompany him even though I was a foot taller than he was. My mother picked out my dress, pink cotton, with a wide, full skirt, fitted waist and short puffy sleeves. The hem was below my knees and not much higher than my flat white shoes. More like a birthday dress than a prom dress. Yet, it was my first real date even if only to the school gym.

Dressed for the big dance, 12 years old.

Not only did my parents take pictures when George picked me up, but we had to stop at his house for his parents to take pictures, too. The teachers were chaperones as a disc jockey played records for us to dance to. Neither of us was much of a dancer. George's main hobby was chess. Mine was reading and playing piano.

George was really not my type, and the courtship did not develop, although our friendship did. I actually had a crush on a muscle-bound hunk I met in my dummy class, Stephen, also an immigrant. We hung out together at parties on Friday nights. There was always music on a record player and dancing. To my chagrin, I had the earliest curfew. At many of these parties, I would hide out in a remote corner of the apartment with a telephone, begging my mother to let me stay longer. No parties on Saturday night because it was hockey night in Canada; if you did not have a ticket, you watched it on television.

Stephen was not my beau for long. When I went to the middle school at Strathcona Academy, I met another boy, Tommy, who would become my steady. He was tall, slim and good looking and his proficiency in English and French grew at about the same pace as mine. His family was part of the wave of 200,000 Hungarians who fled the military crackdown by the Soviet Union, following the failed uprising in 1956.

My grandmother strongly disapproved of the friendship. "Romanians and Hungarians have been enemies for centuries," she explained. Tommy and I did not feel the same way.

Often, we worked on our studies together, by telephone as I sat in our hall closet or on my balcony while Tommy sat on the fire escape of the building across the way. As I was the better student, he came to rely on me for homework and test preparation because he had ambitions to go to medical school. We were going steady by the time we got to ninth grade in Outremont High School.

My mother's colleagues were also a large influence on my work life. They all beamed with pride when I was hired at Woolworth's at the age of fourteen, for a few hours on Saturdays, straightening out the comic book section. The next year, I was selling ice cream sandwiches, which I constructed by layering toasted, previously frozen waffles and identically sized, thin rectangular slices of Neapolitan ice cream. The entire operation was set up on a table just outside the store where I had a freezer and cash register. I felt like an entrepreneur!

They were even more proud of me when I started to attend college, still working at Woolworth's at seventeen although by then I was a supervisor. They all attended my sweet sixteen and eventually my bridal shower.

By the time my mother started working for Woolworth's, my father had developed his own business as a jobber, a wholesale merchant. He picked up fruits and vegetables at the farmers' market very early in the morning for delivery to various delicatessens, diners and restaurants, most of which were owned by our fellow immigrants—the Greeks. My father never actually learned to speak English but he did become conversant in Greek.

It was backbreaking work but my father didn't complain as he had with his factory job. He liked being his own boss, regardless of whether he was actually making any money. Whenever he had some extra cash, he would bring gifts home for my mother—a vacuum cleaner, a fur hat, a crystal vase. Unfortunately, his business acumen was no better in Montreal than it had been in Israel.

I never really understood why we left Israel until we were in Montreal where I saw my father struggling once again in his own business. The problem in Israel was that the hundreds of thousands of war refugees who managed to make their way there, arrived penniless. There was little money in the economy. A lot of my father's grocery sales were on credit because he had no choice. People had to eat. But they had no ability to pay their debts. As a result, my parents couldn't pay their own debts. When we left in the middle of the night, secretly, we were running away from creditors. I never knew why my father went bankrupt in Montreal, but I suspect it was a similar issue—an inability to collect on bad debt.

It was when Sandu started to struggle again when I was about 12-13 that I started to understand what was going on. I knew he was struggling because my mother would ask whether he brought money home and he would say, "no." She would then ask whether there would be money the next day and he would avoid answering her. Their accountant started to come to the apartment. By then I was part of the discussions acting as a translator and (strategist!) for my father and grandmother as well as my mother. Sandu went bankrupt around then, and a second time after my wedding. My mother was always the main wage earner, supporting my grandmother and the three of us on her Woolworth's salary.

I think he was beaten down by one failure after another and living with a wife who did not seem to love him. Sandu felt a defeated man and became very unhappy. He began to drink a lot, coming home very drunk a few times a week. Although he was a happy drunk, my mother nagged him about his drinking until he became so furious he wildly threw something across the living room. One time it was the crystal vase. It shattered into a million pieces. Whatever joy he got out of drinking quickly dissipated.

Shortly after I was married, he finally gave up and went back to selling shoes, the trade he had been taught by my mother's father, Carol. Sandu found a job in a fashionable shoe store on St. Catherine Street, Montreal's famous downtown shopping district. When I visited him there, he took great pleasure in helping me try on a shoe. He slipped the shoe onto my foot, with the broadest smile I had seen in years. His happiness was palpable. I knew that he finally found some peace of mind.

Chapter Seven

SUMMER CAMP

FOR MANY THOUSANDS of immigrants arriving in Montreal in
the 1950s and 1960s, summer camp afforded their children the
opportunity to enjoy the Canadian outdoors, an integral part of
the Canadian identity. Camp also gave hardworking immigrants the
chance to have their children cared for during the months between
school terms.

Before sleep-away camp, I spent two summers in Neighborhood
House's rowdy day camp, a staple of the immigrant community.
Housed in an old brick multi-story structure on a corner of St.
Lawrence Street, Neighborhood House was not only affordable but
also close to the grocery store where my mother was working.

But, by the time I was thirteen, my mother had saved enough
money to send me to sleep-away camp. I loved Camp B'nai B'rith. The
two-hour bus trip from Montreal took us north into the Laurentian
Mountains. We girls sang camp songs the entire way and were fast
friends before we even arrived.

B'nai B'rith was set amidst lush vegetation, all variety of evergreens
and maple trees flanking a lake with a gravel path that meandered from
the green painted wooden mess hall down to the lake and then up to

bunkhouses set in the woods across the way. You could hear the soft wind rustling leaves and smell the fresh woody scent of pine needles. In front of the mess hall was a gathering spot around the flagpole on which both the Canadian and Israeli flags waved in the breeze. One of my favorite parts of the day was the raising of the flags, with everyone assembled to sing both the Canadian and Israeli anthems. In the evening while the flags were being lowered, we also sang "Taps" in Hebrew—a reminder of better times for me.

It was at sleep-away camp that I re-discovered my Judaic roots; since my religious education had been largely ignored since we'd left Israel, I even learned an important prayer, the blessing after the meal, which we never said at home

In Israel, religion is embedded in the fabric of everyday life. Israelis, some more than others, lived by religious tenets. Israel's laws and social institutions arise directly out of the Jewish interpretation of the Old Testament, the Torah. Hebrew was the dominant language. All business ceased on Shabbat. In school, we studied the Bible as an historical text. I never needed to go to after-school Hebrew school in Montreal, as other children did to learn about the Jewish faith and their Jewish roots.

The First Amendment to the American Constitution is interpreted to provide a separation between Church and State. But in fact, in deference to the dominant Church, all businesses are closed on Christmas except of course, Chinese restaurants and movie theaters. Canada's Constitution is different and although religious freedom is protected, Catholicism reigns in Quebec. For years, I listened to so much glorious music for weeks before Christmas that I knew the words to all of the popular holiday carols. "Oh Holy Night, the stars are brightly shining, it is the night of our dear Savior's birth," was among my favorites. The music is beautiful and inspiring and I still enjoy singing it. If my grandmother knew what I was singing, she would turn over in her grave.

I never really thought I was missing out on religious training until I got to camp in Montreal, where the others all knew so many more rituals and songs. It seemed strange to me that religious instruction was available here to children of other faiths as well, since formal instruction was never deemed necessary in Israel.

Camp was special in other ways. At home, I was surrounded by adults. At camp, I could escape into the life that I imagined others had with brothers and sisters. I cherished the companionship and camaraderie of the bunkhouse. "This is what it must be like to live with siblings," I thought.

One year, I read and fell in love with Margaret Mitchell's best-selling novel *Gone With the Wind*. Quite a metamorphosis for a girl in the dummy class, to go from *Dick and Jane* to *Gone With the Wind* in four years!

Every night, after lights out, with the aid of my trusty flashlight, I would read parts of the book out loud to the rest of my bunkmates for as long as I could. "Put the book away," one of the counselors from outside the bunkhouse would have to yell. "Lights out now." I do not remember when I first saw the movie on TV, but it is still vivid for me. Both the book and the movie have all the necessary ingredients of a heart-rending romantic saga—love, war, a love triangle, and tragedy—with an unconventional ending. In reality, it is a story of survival—not altogether unlike our family story, with strong women at its heart.

"As God is my witness, I'll never go hungry again." I still find it such dramatic dialogue, though maybe a little dated and silly.

Chapter Eight

ATLANTIC CITY

IN THE SPRING of 1965, as Montreal melted the last of its black snow, we reached a milestone. My parents studied; they took a test. Then, one day, I put on the powder blue sweater my mother bought me for my birthday and the matching short, A-line skirt I had sewn.

Instead of going to school, I took the bus with my parents to some official building (with an elevator!) on Drummond Street, later renamed Rue Renée Levesque after the French Minister of Quebec who was elected during the separatist battles of the 1960s and 1970s.[1]

"We are citizens!" proclaimed my parents on the elevator back down. As naturalized citizens of Canada, we now could travel to the States without a visa. This was a big deal for immigrants, war refugees really, still looking for a permanent home since being displaced by World War II. I say we—but it was really our parents—a lost generation after the War.

---

1. The Separatist Movement was responsible for a huge exodus of Jews from Quebec Province, particularly Montreal, significantly shifting the balance of English and French speakers and voters. Much of the City's wealth migrated, too, to other parts of Canada, mostly Toronto.

My Canadian Citizenship photo,
15 years old.

That spring, my mother gave me a choice about my summer plans after she explained, "We now can go to America because we no longer need a visa to go to the States. What do you say? Instead of camp, let's go to the ocean this year. It will be just the two of us. Maybe you will meet a nice boy," my mother said, ignoring the fact that I was already "going steady." More importantly, she added, "We will be able to go to the ocean, just as we did in Israel."

My mother also explained that there was not enough money for me to go to both sleep-away camp and to Atlantic City, her first choice. And there would not be enough money for my father and grandmother to accompany us. I could choose one or the other.

What did I know about Atlantic City? It was in New Jersey where every year they televised the Miss America Pageant. There was a boardwalk and the Atlantic Ocean. On TV it looked like a fun place. I would be giving up three weeks of camp for five days in the sunshine. B'nai B'rith would still be there next year. Although I loved camp and had a steady boyfriend, the enticement of the ocean and meeting new boys was irresistible. I chose Atlantic City.

It had not been easy for my mother to leave my father who preferred to keep her at his constant beck and call. But, she was determined to go and taking me on a vacation was an acceptable excuse.

On a hot July morning, my mother and I found ourselves in Atlantic City's crowded bus terminal as the sun streamed in through large windows. Atlantic City was then Montreal's number one travel destination, particularly for Jewish immigrants. The number of Quebec license plates on the Garden State Parkway still bears witness to the many Quebecois who like to travel to the Jersey shore, although Wildwood is now the preferred destination.

On our Greyhound bus, a traveling tube of humanity with its own rules of etiquette, (such as, one must not extend an arm beyond the arm-rest and intrude into someone else's space), we tossed and turned all night in our narrow, uncomfortable seats. A short customs break at the Canadian border and then again a brief stop in Saratoga Springs, allowed us to stretch our legs. In New York's Port Authority, we boarded another Greyhound.

Sleepy and dazed after the overnight Greyhound bus rides, we planned our next move. We must have made quite a sight; my mother, a pretty though heavyset woman in her midlife and I, her physically mature 15-year-old daughter, both of us tastefully overdressed in dark, long pants and matching button down blouses. I was carrying my first purse, a small, compact navy blue leather bag with shoulder strap, given to me only a few months earlier by my best friend for my birthday. Amid the oppressive heat and the morning rush of honking cabs and people hurriedly making their way to their destinations, I suddenly smelled the refreshing salt air. It was such a welcome, familiar smell, reminiscent of my happy childhood on the Mediterranean. I could not wait to get to the beach. My mother tightly clutched our confirmed reservation for a room in the New Yorker Hotel.

With determination, we made our way through the crowd to one of the waiting taxis whose driver was incredulous that we were going to the New Yorker Hotel. "No one under the age of 70 stays at the New Yorker," said the cab driver. "Do you want me to take you to another hotel?"

"No. We want to go to the New Yorker," said my mother. Having survived a war and two immigrations by her wits, she was not about to fall prey to some shifty taxi driver. She insisted on being driven to the hotel recommended by our elderly landlord. After all, it was supposed to be a reputable, kosher hotel where he himself had stayed numerous times. She figured that we would be safe there among our fellow Jews.

The taxi driver took us to 128 South Connecticut Avenue to the New Yorker and waited, watching curiously, as the hotel's matronly owner greeted us. "Come in; come in" said Mrs. Gabby Wolfson, imploring us joyfully, amazed to see young guests at her door. "Your daughter will have a great time here," she assured my mother. "I have two young, handsome Jewish waiters she will love to meet. Herm is in Philadelphia today. He had to go to register for the military draft. But his friend, Irv, is here and I will introduce you to him at dinner."

After mulling it over between us and seeing that the room was nicely appointed and clean, my mother and I decided to stay for at least one night. It would give us time to explore the city and to find other accommodations. Besides, we felt sorry for Mrs. Wolfson.

And so it was that on July 9, 1965, in the fading light of the early evening, my mother and I strolled down the Atlantic City boardwalk for the first time. We ran into Irv, the waiter whom we had met at dinner. I liked Irv but was not attracted to him. But he was standing on the boardwalk next to a tall, slim and handsome young man whom he introduced that same evening as his friend and fellow waiter Herm, who had just come back.

Herm was eighteen years old, with a muscular build, wearing a short-sleeved, button down shirt with tight black denim pants. I was intrigued by his handsome chiseled face and Romanesque nose. His olive, tanned skin complimented his crystal clear blue eyes and emphasized his captivating smile. His resemblance to Paul Newman in the poster for the movie *Hud*, which hung in my bedroom at the time, was uncanny—at least to me.

I have no memories of what the pleasantries were, but I was immediately smitten, and so was he. Although I already had a steady boyfriend at home, I no longer cared—after all, I was only fifteen and what happened on vacation didn't count—or so it was in the movies.

The next morning during breakfast, I watched Herm doing his work in the dining room. I noticed his beautiful hands, long fingers with clean, well-shaped nails, hands that would prove to be strong but gentle. Herm was no speed demon; but slowly, methodically, he went about his duties. He poured coffee, delivered plates of food, and bussed the tables.

He served lunch in much the same way. After lunch was over and all the other guests left, I stayed behind in the dining room, hoping to attract his attention. As Herm made his way from table to table, clearing each one and setting it for the next meal, I followed him around unabashedly, waiting for him to make a move. We made idle conversation as he went about his chores. Still no speed demon, he was undoubtedly mulling over how to go about asking me out. Eventually, he had the good sense to invite me to the beach with him later that afternoon, during his break. We were certainly on the same wavelength.

On the Boardwalk in Atlantic City.

We went to the beach near the hotel, right off Connecticut Avenue's intersection with the Boardwalk. Since it was a Thursday, it was not too crowded, but there were plenty of people enjoying the sand, sea, and air. I don't remember it being very hot but maybe that was just a function of my youth. I do recall jumping the waves with Herm before we plopped down on a blanket on the hot sand. Then I seductively put on my lipstick, as I'd probably seen in some Elvis Presley teen movie. This time he was a speed demon, gently saying as he leaned into me, "Let's see how that lipstick tastes." Pretty corny, but sweet.

After that first date on the beach, Herm and I were inseparable for the balance of my five-day vacation. In the dining room, he continued waiting on my mother and me. Obviously, we never did find the need to go looking for another hotel. My mother joked that, "Herm had better find another way to make a living because he served our soup with his fingers inside the bowl."

Herm quipped back, "I guess that's why you only left a $5 tip for the week."

After lunch, I'd hang around the dining room until it came time for us to go to the beach. After dinner, I waited until Herm finished clearing, setting, and sweeping so we could walk the Boardwalk. One evening, we even got special permission from my mother for a later curfew so that we could go to the movies to see *What's New Pussycat?*, Woody Allen's debut comedy with Peter Sellers and Peter O'Toole. The dialogue was so far over my head, I don't think I understood the movie until about twenty years later. But the plot didn't really matter. I was just so happy to be out with Herm. The title song, belted out by Tom Jones, became our song.

On another day, while we were out for a walk, a sudden, torrential rainstorm soaked us as we ran back to the hotel. Innocently, I invited Herm to our room to dry off. My mother walked in while we were toweling ourselves. She was horrified. "What are you doing?" she bellowed.

"We came back to dry off because we got soaking wet," I sputtered.

"I don't care if you are wet. You cannot have a boy in our room under any circumstance."

In anger and fear, she turned to Herm and demanded, "You get out of here right now!"

I later learned from Herm that he felt wronged by her reaction. He never had any bad intentions. In addition, he told me that on his way out the wind caught the door and it loudly slammed shut. I don't think either my mother or I noticed this at the time but Herm worried all that night that my mother thought he had slammed it in a fit of anger.

I soon learned that despite the maternal dramatics, my mother actually liked Herm—"a nice Jewish boy"—and had secretly accepted our explanation about the rain.

The following weekend, three days after we met, Herm's brother, Lenny, came to the beach to see his little brother and have a little fun. Atlantic City was also Jewish Philadelphia's favorite summer destination. Nine years older than Herm, Lenny was in his late 20s and newly divorced. Though not as tall as Herm, Lenny too was pretty svelte with an olive complexion, thick head of dark hair, and the same enchanting blue eyes. He did not seem to have any problem attracting the ladies.

The three of us spent most of Saturday afternoon together, lying on the beach, talking, joking and jumping into the ocean every once in a while to cool off. Always a charming storyteller, Lenny told a joke I still remember about a Jewish radio station that announced, "1210 on the a.m. dial, but for you, 1200." I enjoyed being with the two brothers, who were very close despite their age difference. Quickly, Lenny sensed that Herm and I had something going. Ever the responsible one, he called home to alert his parents to a potential development.

After all the hardships Moishe and Pesche had known, when I met them in 1965, times were relatively good. They were working in a grocery store they owned, but not as hard as they had in the past. Every other week, alternating with their partner, they took two days off from work.

Lenny had already graduated from Drexel Institute of Technology with a degree in mechanical engineering and was working for a large-equipment company. Herm had just graduated from high school and would be starting college at Temple University in the fall as a psychology major.

Herm and his friend, Irv, decided to celebrate their high school graduation with a summer of freedom in Atlantic City. It was a place where they had gone many times as youngsters for sun and fun, a place they knew would have lots of work for them in its numerous hotels and restaurants. Their plan was to get summer jobs as waiters, spend as little as possible on a room at the Sun-Fun Manor, and spend their free time picking up girls.

Lenny thought his parents would be concerned about Herm's life being complicated by a girl. It did not seem a problem to us, but for Herm and Lenny's parents, Pesche and Moishe, who had dedicated their lives to their sons' education and well-being and had seen Lenny forgo further post-graduate education for marriage, it seemed like a "tragedy" waiting to happen. They firmly believed as all immigrants

Probably what Herm's parents saw.

did that a college education was an immigrant's ticket to success. They did not want anything to stand in Herm's way. Herm's falling in love with a girl from Canada seemed even more problematic and would create unpredictable difficulties. Moishe and Pesche were so concerned that they were soon on the way to Atlantic City to investigate the "crisis" for themselves.

Moishe and Pesche arrived together on Monday, the day my mother and I were leaving. We met only briefly outside the New Yorker Hotel. Herm's father was wearing long pants and a short sleeved white shirt, his face red and flushed from the heat because he was so fair. I examined Moishe's face closely in the bright sunlight and noticed a resemblance to Herm, the same bright blue eyes and a shy, devilish smile. Pesche, with a round, full face and olive skin wore a colorful tight fitting dress that showed off her small waist and large bosom. They were friendly and courteous to both my mother and me. I did not pick up any budding hostility. The true extent of their disapproval was never and will never be known to me, but their immediate reaction, I later learned, was to nag Herm relentlessly about the disadvantages of a long distance relationship.

Herm and I had had a tender and difficult separation the night before, promising to maintain contact and to write often. Before my mother and I climbed into Moishe's car, a blue 1961 Chevrolet, for a ride back to the Greyhound Bus Station, Herm and I exchanged photographs. On the back of Herm's high school graduation picture, which I carry in my wallet to this day, he wrote the following:

The photo Herm gave me and his
inscription on the back.

I was too pre-occupied with the business of traveling to think or feel much. I was confident that Herm and I would see each other again. Herm did not wait for our bus to leave. In his first letter, he wrote, "I'm sorry I didn't stay to see your bus leave, but I guess I just wasn't thinking correctly. I didn't think it would happen, but tears began to form in my eyes when I said good-bye to you. That must be a good sign."

The optimism of youth is such a good thing.

My daughters, who met and married their husbands in their later twenties thought it absurd that parents would be concerned about an 18-year-old son's five-day-old relationship. But given the family's history, struggles, fears and hopes, and their strong involvement in their children's lives, I didn't find it so surprising. Polish Jews who had survived the Holocaust, Siberian exile and four years in camps for Displaced Persons, Moishe and Pesche had come to the U.S. with almost nothing but their indomitable good will, determination to succeed, no matter how much hard work it took, and two small sons whose future meant everything to them.

I sometimes wonder what life would have brought had I chosen sleep-away camp over Atlantic City that summer. Were Herm and I fated to meet, if not there and then, somewhere else? Sometimes I believe we were meant to be together, would be together, regardless.

Chapter Nine

Long Distance

THE FIRST THING I did when I returned to Montreal was break up with my steady boyfriend. When I told Tommy and my best friend Kathy about this wonderful boy I'd met, I said he was not only handsome, but considerate, soft-spoken, and mature. A rare find. I never had a relationship with anyone in which I was made to feel like we were equals. I certainly never saw it at home or was treated that way by Tommy. He had never valued my opinion about anything. Herm cared about what I had to say and about how I felt. I never saw Herm angry.

Tommy showed little reaction although I knew he felt hurt for which I genuinely felt bad. He refused to show that I'd hurt his feelings. Overtly, his attitude was to discount my story. Consequently, no one believed me. My friends thought I'd invented him. Even seeing Herm's picture didn't convince them my story was real. I don't know why they would think I would make such a thing up. I wasn't prone to tall tales, lying or showing off. But, I must admit, sometimes, I didn't believe it myself. It seemed too good to be true even to me—that in a few short days, my whole world had changed completely. At those times, doubts arose about whether we would ever see each other again. Was it just a summer fling for Herm?

Herm had the sense to suggest a letter-writing schedule, to help us sustain a long distance relationship without putting too much pressure on either of us. We each wrote every two weeks. So, one week I would write a letter, and the following week I would receive a letter. To make the endless two-week interval bearable, we planned to call one another. We also planned to see one another next during my school Christmas break, less than five months away.

In Atlantic City, my mother and I had borrowed a small, transistor radio and an old blanket from Herm. When it came time to leave, we left these on a chair in the lobby for him to retrieve. As Canadians, we trusted they would not be stolen but alas, the radio went missing. In his first letter, Herm gently suggested that we check our luggage to see if we had "accidentally placed my radio somewhere." I was mortified that he might think we'd taken it, and immediately responded with a short letter and a check to cover the cost of the radio.

Just after I mailed the letter, the Canadian postal workers went on a wildcat strike. It felt like a personal affront. "How could they do this to me?" I wailed. It was the first strike of its kind in Canada. Now my letter was stuck in the mail.

The illegal strike organized when postal employees' workloads doubled without a corresponding increase in wages, was the first of many more crippling postal strikes over the years of our long-distance courtship. Worried that my letter would never reach Herm, I agonized over what to do. "Should I call? He'll think I'm chasing him." In those days, it was unheard of for a girl to phone a boy, especially one she'd known for such a short time. But if I didn't? I couldn't let him think that I hadn't written back.

I decided to give it a try since I had a valid excuse, a good reason. I had to tell him I'd sent a check for the radio. I was no thief.

To heighten the drama—and my anxiety—I couldn't reach him on the lone telephone at the Sun-Fun Manor, where he and Irv were renting a room. But once I'd made the decision to call, I wasn't going to give up easily. I tried the New Yorker Hotel but he wasn't there, either. I had no choice but to leave a message with the owner, Mrs. Wolfson. She was not only very cooperative and supportive, but actually insistent that she would relay the message. I know she liked Herm very much, and she took full credit for our relationship. "Such a nice Jewish boy, and handsome, too," she reminded me, as if I needed reminding.

It was his friend Irv who called me back. He explained that Herm was not at work because he was too sick to work. "What? Herm is sick? First, the radio, then the mail, now sick? What else is going to interfere with this relationship?" I asked the Almighty.

Herm, though I didn't know it yet, was a first-class ruminator himself. When he received my message, he worried that if he didn't return the call quickly enough, I would get the wrong idea about his interest in me. He was never comfortable with ambiguity.

That evening, in the middle of one of New Jersey famous Nor'easters, and quite ill with bronchitis, he dragged himself to a boardwalk pay phone to call me. He could barely hear me over the howling wind and pounding rain as I explained, "I wrote you a letter, but it is stuck in the mail."

"Don't worry. I understand," he said.

"I am so sorry I got you out of bed."

"I'm not really that sick," he tried to reassure me. "Just bronchitis. A little rest and the antibiotics will take care of it." I felt relief. Our relationship would continue despite these minor setbacks. And I thanked the Almighty.

Despite the post office strikes, a couple of letters did make it through the mail. In the first, Herm returned the money I had sent for the radio. I used it to pay for a couple of our long distance calls—very expensive in those days. In his next letter, he said, "As usual, it was heavenly speaking to you on the phone." He also expressed frustration at our being apart. "I'm afraid to go to sleep because I immediately begin to dream about us, and I've had so many dreams that they're driving me crazy. (Who wants to dream? I want the real thing!!)." I was having the same dreams.

As the summer came to an end, I still felt even closer and more attached to Herm. How I longed to see him again! In every one of our letters, we expressed an urgency to be together again, my Christmas break was still four months away.

Then, unexpectedly, in mid-August, Herm wrote he would be coming to Montreal. Moishe and Pesche decided to go along with Herm's wish—"Since I came home from A.C., that's all we discussed. I'm happy to report that it looks pretty definite that we'll be coming up." It would be a family vacation before Labor Day.

I was surprised and elated when Herm told me he was coming, although doubly surprised that his parents would accompany him. It caused a stir in our household—a flurry of cleaning, baking and cooking broke out in preparation for out of town guests. We know that to honor their being kosher meant we would be eating all our meals in. I remember singing and dancing my way around the apartment in anticipation, as any starry-eyed 15-year-old would do. At the same time, I felt very uneasy about what his family would think of mine. Herm was so ecstatic he could barely contain himself in a long, romantic letter he wrote, "This week has been so exciting for me that I don't know if I'll be able to last until I see you…. It's going to be strange to see you after all these weeks. I hope you haven't changed, because you were just fine when I saw you."

What could he be talking about? Did I change? With him, I felt more like myself than I had in all the years since we had come to Canada.

After a couple of weeks of anticipation, Herm and his parents drove the three hundred and sixty-five miles along winding Route 9 to Montreal, long since replaced by the New York Thruway and Adirondack Northway. They came directly to our apartment, where they met my grandmother and my father, "Your parents were simply great and so nice to me," wrote Herm later. "And your grandmother is so sweet, I think she's my favorite." She certainly was my favorite.

Herm slept on a sofa-bed in the living room of our three-bedroom apartment while his parents stayed in a motel on Decarie Boulevard near Ruby Foo's much more elegant accommodations.

Our two families shared meals at home since Herm's family never violated their commitment to eating kosher food. We sat at a folding table that had been set up in the living room. The yellow Formica and aluminum kitchen table was too small in a crowded space. My mother and grandmother prepared their Romanian specialties, including stuffed cabbage, breaded chicken, pickles, and eggplant salad. For dessert, my mother made her chocolate chiffon swirl cake. She was not much of a baker, but she had mastered that one cake.

We did all our sightseeing in Herm's parents' car. My parents never owned a car. I am sure I was not the best tour guide since we had arrived in the country only five years earlier, and English was my third language. We took them to the top of Mount Royal, a vantage point from where you could see the city rise out of the St. Lawrence River, and took lots of pictures. In those days, no skyscrapers dominated the skyline. One could see the grain storage silos and flour factories on the edge of the water, where two years later Expo '67 would be built. We also walked around Beaver Lake on which Montreal children and adults alike come to skate during the winter months.

Although the visit was short, just one week, all seven of us—my mother, father and grandmother, Herm and his parents, and I piled into their car (no seatbelts back then), and spent a day driving up to the town of St. Agathe-des-Monts, a popular summer retreat in the Laurentian Mountains. The town lies on a large lake, Lac des Sables, on which many French and English speaking families, many Jewish people among them, built pretty summer cottages that dotted the evergreen-rich shoreline.

It was a lovely late summer day, with a chill in the air so common at that time of the year, rich with the fragrant smell of pines. Summer is so short in Canada. We brought along our own picnic lunch and strolled down a tree-lined path in one of St. Agathe's parks. In a surviving 8-millimeter home-movie, taken with Lenny's movie camera, our two families are making our way together toward the photographer. Herm is walking alongside me, with his arm comfortable around my shoulders. Suddenly, Moishe reaches over and plants a juicy kiss on my cheek, the first of many more to come.

"My plan worked," Herm still boasts. His instincts were good. Unbeknownst to me, a plan to end our relationship when it had barely begun had been lurking in the background. Over the summer Herm's parents had become increasingly concerned about the "catastrophe" of their son getting involved with a girl just before starting college. Finally, they insisted he break it off. Deftly avoiding conflict, he repeatedly assured them that he would break up with me before starting college. Then, as college got closer and closer, he slyly explained to his parents, "I can't just break up with her in a letter or over the phone. I can only manage this in person."

What I also didn't know yet was that Herm was born an expert nagger. His brother used to call him "the nag" and make fun of him. "Ich vil drivin!" ("I want to drive!" in Yiddish), was reportedly such an oft-heard whine when he was a 10-year-old that Lenny while driving would finally let him sit on his lap holding the steering wheel. It took me some time to realize that, as gentle and people-pleasing as Herm seems to be, he has an uncanny way of relentlessly nagging, until resistance is futile and he gets his way. His parents never had a chance in this debate.

During the brief visit, our two families shared backgrounds and values became apparent, as did the obvious joy on our faces. In his next letter, Herm wrote, "The week I spent in Montreal, I think was the nicest week I've ever spent." Ever a romantic, he enclosed part of a composition written by one of his classmates for their yearbook:

It was then, when the shapeless Indefinite hugged the earth, that we touched. Our hands, our lips, our hearts met and fought solitude. When the sky lost its eyes, we saw. We looked at our teardrops and laughed. We heard the footsteps of Love when night kissed the day, so we knew that the battle was won; we were one.

Needless to say, Herm did not break up with me.

Chapter Ten

THE COURTSHIP

CONTINUED

FOUR MONTHS LATER, my mother and I once again boarded a
Greyhound bus for the nightlong torture-ride to New York. Herm and
I had seen each other twice in the previous six months, including the
late August visit one on my turf. It was time to see whether we could
maintain the same level of attraction on his turf.

At the Port Authority Bus Terminal my mother and I transferred
to the Philadelphia bus and traveled along the New Jersey Turnpike,
which lived up to its reputation as an unsightly and smelly route. It
ran along numerous pig farms not to mention oil storage and refining
facilities. It is still the major throughway between New York City and
Delaware. Fortunately, it has now been divided into two roadways,
with a separate one for trucks, which reduces the likelihood of being
killed by one. Whenever I mention to anyone from out of state that
I live in New Jersey, inevitably, I'm asked, "What exit?" I have yet to
figure a short way to answer that question because we live in Western
New Jersey, twenty miles west of the turnpike.

Philadelphia's 30th Street Station was much grander than Atlantic
City's bus station. The view was breathtaking. The arrival gates

were more distinctive and emptied into a vast terminal, lined with multiple-story columns reaching for a high domed ceiling. There were many important-looking people crisscrossing the ornate lobby. Most were more formally dressed than Canadians. Also, coming from Canada, my mother was particularly surprised by the large number of African-Americans in the crowd. It was the height of the civil rights movement. Canadian television news had been filled with the politically charged and violent reverberations of the marches in Selma and Washington. My mother was scared.

Like other Canadian teens, I was just as enamored of the Kennedy presidency as teens in the U.S. and strongly supported the civil rights movement. However, older Jews, such as my parents and future in-laws, all too familiar with prejudice and racial violence, were frightened by the rise in unrest. It wasn't easy for my mother to get comfortable walking around the city.

Herm met us at the station, where we had a heart-felt and joyous reunion although I felt shy for the first few minutes. He then took us to our motel on City Line Avenue across from the Bala Cynwyd Shopping Center, near his parents' apartment on the corner of Euclid Avenue, not far from the busy intersection of 54th Street and City Line Avenue. Once again, as he had in his letters, Herm tried to persuade us to stay with his family, but my mother would never dream of imposing and insisted on a motel.

Herm picked us up to go to dinner at their apartment, a three-story rental building in a neighborhood of mixed housing, including single homes. Their apartment was one flight above a tailor shop, quite small, but bright and modestly and tastefully furnished.

We entered through the small living room, furnished with a sofa and armchair, the cushions of both covered in plastic, an iconic decorating feature of the time. The sofa was tucked under a large window on the street side. On the opposite side, the living room opened into a dining room, dominated by an oval table and chairs with plastic covered seats, also home to a birdcage for Herm's parakeet Mickey. Diagonally to the left was a small kitchen and to the right were two bedrooms and a bathroom. Moishe and Pesche's bedroom was surprisingly furnished with an art deco, gray lacquer bedroom set. Herm and Lenny shared the other small bedroom, with twin beds on either side of a night table.

Highly polished silver candlesticks sparkled on the dining room table and chandelier lights twinkled into the brightly lit room. Everything was impeccably clean, and delicious smells wafted in from the kitchen.

We shared a wonderful meal prepared by Pesche. She was a great cook and introduced me to new Jewish foods, like chicken soup with "knadelach" (matzo balls), a mainstay of Eastern European Jewish cuisine quite different from the Romanian fare I had grown up on. The conversation between my mother and Herm's parents was lively, but neither Herm nor I said much as we surreptitiously surveyed each other, communicating with meaningful glances and facial expressions. I was dying to touch and hold Herm but I behaved myself, confident we would have time the next day.

Herm borrowed his parents' car to drive my mother and me on our first day back together, of course, touring some of Philadelphia's popular sites. We drove down City Line Avenue, all sharing the front

On the steps of the Hubers' apartment, winter, 1966.

bench seat of the Chevy—my mother couldn't sit in the back? We made our way to West River Drive where Herm pointed out the crew clubhouses lining the banks of the Schuylkill River and ended at the Philadelphia Art Museum. He pointed out the original museum was chartered for the 1876 Centennial World's Fair but was not completed until 1928. Its famous steps would later be featured in the *Rocky* movies.

Herm enjoyed showing us around and I enjoyed listening to his soft voice as we drove through Fairmount Park; he explained that the park was host to the 1876 Centennial Exhibition, a grand celebration of 100 years of American independence as well as cultural and industrial progress. It was the first major World's Fair in the United States and introduced Alexander Graham Bell's telephone to the world.

We continued gawking at the beautiful old buildings and Civil War memorials with little understanding of their relevance, but impressed nonetheless by them and the charming Japanese pagoda with its gardens. Downtown, we drove around City Hall, atop which nobly rested a statue of William Penn; this was Philadelphia's tallest structure, which no other building was permitted to surpass in height, at the time. Herm pointed out the Franklin Institute and the Philadelphia Library, another majestic structure. "I spent many days at the library when I played hooky," he explained. We also paid our respects to the Monument to the Six Million Jewish Martyrs.

The following day, when we were finally able to spend time by ourselves, we walked through Fairmount Park, holding hands and really feeling comfortable in each other's company. As we strolled through the park, Herm took pictures and related many of his early adventures there. "I broke my arm climbing on Pegasus," he told me, referring to one of the enormous bronze statues remaining from the World's Fair, surrounded by other equestrian heroes of various wars and revolutions.

"Did I tell you I was bitten by a dog when I was three years old?"

"What? How did that happen?"

"There was a dog running loose. When I tried to pet him, he bit me."

"So, what happened?"

"The police came and searched for the dog. They couldn't find it, so, there was no way to know whether it was rabid. My mother had to take me to the hospital for a series of 21 shots in the abdomen. That was the only known cure for rabies then."

On New Year's Eve, we had dinner with our parents again but afterwards Herm and I left to go to a movie in Ardmore, one of the wealthy suburbs on Philadelphia's famous "Main Line." I wore a pretty, store-bought, white wool dress that stopped just below my knees, despite the frigid night. Herm kept his arm around me as we made our way down the deserted streets of Ardmore. Few people were out despite the holiday. The Ardmore Theater, a Beaux-Arts building opened in 1926 and served as a movie house until 2000. We saw a James Bond movie, *Thunderball* with Sean Connery. I can't remember much about it because, as was often the case, we were romantically occupied in the last row of the theater. After the movies, we sat in the car, in the Bala Cynwyd Shopping Center parking lot directly across from our motel, and ushered in our first new year together, keeping close to keep from shivering to death. There was no other place to go for privacy.

Cozy New Year's dinner with Moishe, Pesche, Netty, and Herm, winter 1966.

The time I spent in Philadelphia ringing in 1966 with Herm
was surreal for me. I felt like I was in another world, where the rules
were different. Certainly, the landscape was new, but also there was no
school, none of my familiar friends. I was free to shed the previous
five years of emotional turmoil and become someone else, someone I
recognized as my true self. Herm and I were still essentially strangers,
learning about each other and carefully feeling our way into a deeper
relationship. Herm talked about how self-conscious he felt about
speaking in public, due to a long struggle with stuttering. I tried to
support him, knowing how it felt to be the object of ridicule, and
reassuring him that he rarely stuttered with me. I confessed how
isolated I felt in Montreal and how much I appreciated his kindness
and gentleness, as compared to the shallowness and macho attitudes of
the other boys I had met.

In the summer of '66, my mother and I returned to Atlantic City
for another beach vacation. Herm met us there, accompanied by his
father. Netty had always loved the beach, which is why she pressed for
Atlantic City in the first place. And I had many memories of Haifa's
white beaches on the Mediterranean Sea. In Haifa, it was often just my
mother and I, sitting on the sand, waiting for the gentle waves to come
crashing over our legs. Light-skinned, I invariably spent many a night
with yogurt on my back to calm the sunburn.

Herm's father, Moishe, did not love the ocean and made a hilarious
sight on the beach. Sitting tucked under an umbrella, with a hat, a
white long sleeved shirt, and a long towel around his legs to protect his
very white skin, he still managed to turn into a beet every day, his face
totally flushed. But, he was a good sport about it.

With my mother on the beach in Haifa when I was 5.

Herm returned to Temple University that fall, and our correspondence continued. He was taking "very hard" courses in religion and philosophy and a fencing class, having been a fencer in high school. In one letter he shared a funny story from his fencing class that I must admit made me a little jealous:

> As you probably know, the main target is the chest, more specifically it corresponds exactly to the breast in a girl. So today we practiced just lunging and hitting the target. Since there are 5 boys and 11 girls in my class, it's almost certain that I get a girl as a partner. Well, I can't tell you. She had to stand there, and I had to hit the target. I was just about always directly on target. I could see she must have felt it pretty well. Meanwhile, I was so embarrassed, you have no idea. People came in from other gym classes just to see this, and I felt so guilty doing it. I felt just as if she was sticking it out, in front of a large audience, and everyone knew what was going on. Anyway, I probably ripped her bra in shreds, and she better come in with an armor-plated one next time. It's funny now (& a little exaggerated), but I was pretty embarrassed then.

Later, he shared again, "P.S. I broke in another girl in fencing class the other day."

Our next meeting was in Montreal, where Herm came for two weeks during his Christmas break. Once again, he stayed in our apartment, sleeping on our living room sofa bed. My parents thought this was quite acceptable, but in retrospect, the inconsistency is glaring. On the one hand, they felt we needed a chaperone. On the other hand, having him in our apartment made it possible for us to spend some intimate moments. My grandmother was appointed our chaperone because my parents were working. However, she was getting pretty old by then, was losing her sight due to diabetes, and was ill equipped to be much of a chaperone. On more than one occasion, we had to quickly change position and reassemble our clothing as we heard her shuffling down the hallway. We couldn't get enough of each other, even though we were trying to be respectful.

From the start, Herm and I felt an intense emotional connection, akin to the kind of uncontrollable love dog lovers feel when—forgive the analogy, they get a new puppy—like a golden retriever puppy. It makes them smile and stare adoringly, all the time. They can't get enough of the puppy. They want to hold and cradle it all the time. They want to play with it even though the puppy's play includes chewing on hands and arms. And slobbering on them. Nothing the puppy does bothers them. That's what it was like for us, except for the slobbering, of course.

It was such a precious time, made even more intense by our frequent long separations. Every time we saw each other it was as if years had passed and no time had passed. When it was time to separate, it became unbearable. Our love deepened and matured, until we could no longer stand living four hundred miles apart.

Chapter Eleven

Separate, but Equal

Lives

When Herm and I met, I was attending highly regarded Outremont High School, built in 1956 to accommodate the large influx of immigrant children, many of whom were intelligent and extremely driven to succeed. At Outremont, after I caught the attention of an astute 9th grade teacher with my advanced skills in sewing and cooking, I finally began making strides in school. Fractions were easy for me to transfer to cutting fabric using a pattern and adjusting for size. The same was true for having to adjust proportions when cooking. Based on her recommendation, I was moved out of the "dummy" class into the college-bound one, which immediately boosted my grades as well as my self-esteem. On the down side, all my classmates changed which heightened my stress levels and made me feel nervous about having to meet higher expectations. I bounced from one extreme to another. One moment, I felt confident I could handle the work, but after making a mistake, I worried about whether I was in over my head. At night, I used to reassure myself that the adults must know what they were doing.

Changing classes meant I was an outsider, trying to fit into already existing cliques, once again, leaving behind friends who helped me through my tentative attempts at assimilation. I gained some social skills at this kind of survival, like how to participate in a conversation even if I didn't understand everything that was being said, but I was hampered by my own feelings of inadequacy. I admire some of the wonderful people I met who did welcome me and did help me fit in, but it was not easy for me. Miss King, my history teacher, spent much extra time teaching me how to research and write a term paper, skills I was never given an opportunity to learn while cooking and sewing. The slow-learners class emphasized practical skills over academic skills. My first history term paper was a huge success—I didn't fail! I might have even done well, but I had not set the bar high.

One day I overheard a conversation between my mother and a teacher at their parent/teacher conference. The teacher insisted, "Based on Ann's behavior in class, Ann is destined to be a follower, not a leader. She does not seem to show initiative or drive to achieve any particular goal. Ann just does the work which is assigned."

"Thank you for telling me the truth," my mother said.

It stunned me and I never forgot it. Netty never discussed it with me and kept this horrid secret to herself. But I didn't believe it to be true. Eventually, a plan formulated itself, without any conscious effort on my part, which drove me to be the best at everything: the way I looked, the way I behaved, the way I excelled in school.

It turned out I was just as driven as the others in this class of striving immigrants—and ultimately just as capable. I joined the Red Cross Chapter where I became the vice-president. I also joined the Library Helpers where I worked my way up to president.

Since around the age of 13 or 14, I had been an avid reader of popular law stories by such authors as Louis Nizer. "I want to be a lawyer," I once announced to my parents.

"Women don't become lawyers," my father scolded. "They become secretaries, nurses, teachers, and librarians."

The Women's Liberation Movement had not yet made its way into the mainstream, but surprisingly my father was an early proponent of women's independence—up to a point. He hammered into me a need to be self-reliant. That meant that I was to be able to take care of myself and support myself, "You should never have to rely on a man," he told me. But this apparently did not mean I could take "a man's job."

As a catalyst for the change in the direction of my personal development, I was getting to know the kindly librarian, Mrs. Anne Galler. Unlike most of my female teachers who were older single women, Mrs. Galler was a pretty, young married woman with a career and two young children. She quickly became my role model. I saw my future: As a librarian, I imagined, I could work and be home for my children during the summer. I dismissed my long-time interest in the law without a second thought, not really thinking about whether I was better suited to the library than the courtroom.

My rise continued steadily. By senior year, I had achieved an appointment to the Leaders Corps, the group of top students who presided at school functions in a special uniform, sporting a green and silver insignia broach and ring, which I still own. I loved wearing the uniform. For me it represented acceptance. While all the students sat in their seats, we walked up and down the aisles, keeping order and helping the teachers.

My self-esteem went up another notch after I was nominated for homecoming queen in my senior year although I ended up as first runner up. I think it was then that I started to believe that no matter how hard I tried, there would always be someone better—a hard pill to swallow for someone who wanted, needed to be the best. Although I did not realize it until I was forty years old and running for our Town Council, these activities were harbingers of my future political aspirations, as were my political conversations with my father. I enjoyed being the center of attention, being listened to and admired.

My father would boast, "My daughter is going to go to McGill." However, my parents didn't know anything about what was necessary

My high school graduation photo, proudly
wearing my Leaders Corps pin, 1967.

to get into college. All they knew was that "McGill University is the best university." Therefore, it was my only option.

After I took the SATs in English and French, it became clear that I would easily be able to gain admission. What would not be so easy for me was to earn a McGill scholarship, which I missed by a few points. I did qualify for a $1,000 provincial scholarship. Considering the first year tuition was $365, it turned out to be a lot of money.

I was disappointed about being unable to get the McGill scholarship but even more disappointing, very hurtful really, was the way I was treated by the Soroptomist International Association, whose stated mission was the support of women's education. Our girls' Vice-Principal, Ms. Thompson took me aside one day and suggested I apply for a scholarship offered by that organization. Together, we filled out the application. Proudly, I wrote to Herm and told him about it.

Months later, Ms. Thompson anxiously pulled me aside again. "I am so sorry to tell you that your application has been denied." She continued, "It was rejected because you are Jewish. I should never have suggested that you try for this one." This so offended my sense of right and wrong that I never forgot the unexpressed anger I felt when I heard the news—my first experience with blatant anti-Semitism. What was the point of even trying when the deck was stacked against me? I learned not to try for things I thought I could not achieve. I would persevere endlessly if I thought something I wanted could be done; but if I had any inkling that there was any institutional bias, I would not even try.

Herm was not there physically to help me deal with the pain of the Soroptomists' rejection. But, in his next letter, he characteristically tried to soften the blow with humor, not fully grasping my distress and disillusionment. "I was disappointed about the Soroptomist thing, and thinking about going down to their office and giving them a piece of my mind, but I decided I couldn't spare a piece. I was already mortally wounded when I saw your SAT scores which were higher than mine."

Being so young and inexperienced, Herm and I thought it might be the mature thing to continue to date others while we were living four hundred miles apart. My friends knew I was completely committed to my relationship with "an American" but I still went to all the dances and dated other boys. Herm did likewise at Temple University, but less so. He took our friend Manya to an ROTC Ball in their freshman year, took her skiing another time where she hurt her knee, and motor-biking a third time when she hurt some other body part. Part of Herm's attraction to me, I think, was that I was quite hardy. One date Herm had arranged, which ultimately fell through, was, "With a beautiful, voluptuous girl but not to worry," he told me, "I am not going to let her get too fresh with me." I never did find out if this was real or not.

I did not disguise my lack of interest in the local and unsophisticated boys at Outremont High School resulting in the following yearbook note:

She is the girl who is forever expecting letters from the States or writing them. Her activities extend from the Red Cross and the Library to sports and the Leaders' Corp. She is always busy, works in her spare time yet manages to be a scholarship student. Ambitious and hard-working she hopes to become a librarian in Philadelphia.

Herm wasn't able to come to my prom but supported my decision to go to the dance with my friend, and former steady boyfriend. He wrote, "Tommy is a better dancer and I don't dance." He did, however, admonish me not to "kiss your date."

I was looking forward to wearing a hand stitched, long, lined green chiffon dress I'd made myself, with a matching green silk wrap. Both later became great dress-up clothes for our daughters.

In retrospect, I'm not sure if our "open" dating idea was really a mature thing or not, but no harm was done to our relationship. Herm and I both came from a family history of few, but serious love relationships. By the time we parted in Atlantic City, something extraordinary had happened to us. We had formed an attachment, a bond, a commitment that remained remarkably stable over a long distance for so long and endured a lifetime.

Still, every separation was increasingly more difficult and as graduation was fast approaching, talk about being together more became inevitable. It seemed only natural to Herm that I should go to college in Philadelphia. I saw no obstacle to such a plan.

My father and mother had other ideas. McGill University would be my only application for 1967. Their only daughter was not going anywhere.

Chapter Twelve

SPRING/SUMMER 1967

ALTHOUGH I WAS a good student and a generally obedient daughter, I rebelled in minor ways. My mother was a weak disciplinarian, often interjecting herself between my father and me. Once, I remember, I went snowmobiling with friends in the Laurentian Mountains and crept home at some ungodly hour. Long before I returned home, my mother had put my boots by the front door so my father would think I was safely tucked in bed.

Innately, she seemed to understand my need to be independent, unconventional, and even a bit oppositional. I wore nylons to school with my uniform even though it was not permitted. I often put on lipstick after the principal's inspection at the school's front door. Though I had an early curfew, I'd always call home and ask to stay out later with one excuse or another. I was not one to live by the rules and in fact, delighted in finding ways to break them.

I frequently violated my curfew, smoked secretly, successfully hid my cigarettes in the mailbox in our building's lobby because it was my job to check the mail, and dated various boys despite my mother's strong disapproval. She didn't understand that both Herm and I had agreed to that arrangement. Nonetheless, I was not prepared to defy my mother or my father by leaving for university in the United States at the age of seventeen. Yet even before my acceptance letter to McGill arrived, Herm was already pestering me about going to school in Philadelphia for my sophomore year. I promised him I would.

Our separations became harder and harder for both of us but especially for Herm. He often complained about being lonely without me and missing me, "All I have to do is study and think about you and maybe watch a little football." I, on the other hand, was pre-occupied with high-school graduation, college, and my future.

The year 1967 was not only a big year for me but for all of Canada. The country was celebrating the centennial of its independence from England, although it was still a member of the British Empire and loyal to the British Crown. As part of the celebration, Montreal hosted the World's Fair, Expo 67, which attracted more than 50 million visitors from all over the world.

Expo 67 opened to huge fanfare in April, a good weather month. Some mornings still carried a chill, but the sun was a welcome sight after the long winter. Everyone was excited about visiting Expo, and the competition for getting a "passport" (ticket) was intense. The passport was also a souvenir booklet for accumulating a stamp of each pavilion's logo. Some pavilions were in much greater demand than others, such as the Russian and the Canadian. We had to stand in line for hours just to pass through them. I was enchanted with the novel architectural wonders such as the U.S.A.'s huge Geodesic Dome, France's Pavilion which has since become Montreal's Casino, and Habitat 67, a revolutionary concept for high density development in an urban setting.

Expo brought the city to life. Most Montrealers visited at least once, and many hosted guests from all over the world. Herm's parents came with their friends, Mr. and Mrs. Leon, and their sons in June. With very sentimental memories, I remember greeting Herm privately.

He held me in a bear hug for a long time while I cried joyful tears to see him again. His parents and their friends were all surprised that a serious relationship had continued between us despite the pressure of long separations.

Since school was over by then, and I only held a part-time job at Woolworth's, I was able to spend most of my time with Herm and his parents at Expo, and my mother joined us. One day we stayed so late, she suddenly became acutely anxious about getting home in time for my father. "I have to get home," she blurted out as she turned and abruptly left the group. I can still picture her, wearing a flowered, sleeveless shift that rustled from side to side as she ran to get on the subway. The Leons commented on her strange behavior for which I could offer no more adequate explanation than, "My father doesn't like it when she's not home, when he returns from work, to make his dinner." I was ashamed to tell them how possessive and jealous he was and how angry he could become.

At the end of their visit, I returned with Herm to Philadelphia for a couple of weeks in what proved to be a turning point in our relationship. We started obliquely talking about marriage, each afraid to use the actual word. We talked about how many children we wanted, about where we would live, and what we thought it would be like to be together for so long. I did not dare bring marriage up directly, thinking it was the man's job to broach the subject. Besides, I thought marriage would be a few years off, after I graduated from college.

As evidence of our increasing endearment to each other, Herm stopped calling me by my name, calling me by a nickname he gave me, Farfel. No clue where it came from, but he has a knack for giving everyone nicknames. Farfel was the first of many nicknames, changing every ten years or so. It later became Farfela, Farf, Pussycat, Little Fella, and more recently Cutie Pie—now on a license plate Herm purchased for my birthday a couple of years ago.

His letter following my visit was funny. He followed every sentence with the words, "I love you." I enjoyed reading his letters immensely. He could never say it too much as far as I was concerned. Though we'd spoken of marriage only obliquely, he also mentioned that Pesche was resigned to the fact that it would be a Montreal wedding. It was a surprise to me that Herm and his parents were talking about marriage plans.

When I returned, I went back to work at Woolworth's and worked at the Expo's Israeli Pavilion cafeteria, too, surely adding to its success. Working both jobs, I saved every penny for college since my parents would not be able to make any contribution to my education. Unlike Moishe and Pesche who had achieved some measure of financial stability, Netty and Sandu lived from paycheck to paycheck. Our financial situation was always a strain. We always lived in an apartment. We never had a car. That's why the vacation to Atlantic City had been such a big deal.

Starting college was so exciting for my mother, grandmother, and me that preparations became a family affair. From my mother and grandmother's perspective, the most important aspect was my wardrobe. With their help, I embarked on sewing an appropriate collection of suits. (In Montreal, jeans had yet to become our generation's uniform.) Following patterns as I had learned in ninth grade, I did the machine sewing; my mother did the fine handwork such as buttons and hems; and my grandmother did the pressing. It was a beehive of activity rivaling the General Motors assembly line.

My father watched from the sidelines with little to contribute, not that we tried to include him, either. He was pretty disillusioned with everything by then, leaving early for work, struggling to make a living, and coming home drunk a few afternoons a week to my mother's dismay. If she did not leave him alone when he came back, it led to a screaming match. I found it best to ignore it.

Walking through the double arches that mark the entrance to McGill University on Sherbrooke Street, in a yellow wool skirt with matching tweed jacket, I felt very mature on my first day of school. I met this new phase of my life with great intensity. I didn't even mind that, in addition to my supervisor's job at Woolworth's, I had to work as a waitress in Victoria Hall, the girls' dorm, where my stomach did summersaults every Sunday serving ham. It remains such a foreign smell to me that I still cannot tolerate it.

I was a commuting student with a financial assistantship as a waitress in the dorm. Unlike the wealthy, suburban students whose parents and grandparents had attended McGill, I was the first one in my family to attend university. My fellow students ignored me as I carried heavily loaded trays to their tables. They never cleaned up after themselves or offered thanks. I was a little resentful at the time but figured it was my lot in life. I didn't have the family connections or the family money to go to college without working. Looking back, I marvel at how condescending my fellow classmates were. Besides waitressing in the dorm and working at Woolworth's that year, I gave private piano lessons to young children, all necessary to make ends meet.

My best friend, Kathy, did not apply to McGill, choosing instead the former Sir George Williams College, now part of Concordia. I was sad that she wasn't there to share the excitement. A number of my former classmates did go to McGill; I had never been totally accepted into their clique in high school. At college, it was easy to abandon them, or maybe they abandoned me, for new friends.

Again, I felt like a fish out of water. So I was thrilled when Herm drove up for a weekend in October. We went out with Kathy and her friend, Elliot, to whom Herm took a liking. The time flew by as we walked and walked miles of the city and spent time around McGill. I had a famous psychology professor, Donald Hebb, whom Herm admired, having studied all about him. He was able to attend one of his lectures, but was disappointed. The lecture was held in a huge classroom with coliseum-style seating and Hebb was a pretty small and boring figure down at the podium.

There was a little café on Sherbrooke where then little-known Leonard Cohen, poet and folksinger, sang. I sometimes went to hear him with friends, but not the weekend Herm was there, unfortunately. Cohen's music appealed to us, though, since he often sang about a lover in Montreal, a haunting song now quite famous: "Suzanne takes you down to her place by the river… She feeds you tea and oranges that come all the way from China… And the sun pours down like honey on our lady of the harbour…." The latter reference is to a statue of a woman atop "Notre-Dame de Bon Secours," a church overlooking the St. Lawrence River shoreline in Old Montreal, blessing the sailors.

Long distance phone calls were very expensive then, so after Herm got back to Philadelphia, he made a person-to-person call to me and asked for himself. This was a signal that he had arrived safely. I told the operator, "There is no one here by that name," and hung up. No charge for outwitting Ma Bell with that little trick. However, Herm later wrote, "Five minutes after I hung up, the operator called me back and asked for Herman Huber. So I figured it was you and I said, 'this is he.' Anyway, she then asked me why I called and asked for myself, and she warned me that it was a violation of some code or other, and that I could be fined for that. Nothing came of it, it was just a warning." It didn't stop us from repeating the trick when necessary.

In one of my classes, I met an American student from Virginia who was also feeling lonely and isolated. We hung out in her apartment, drinking vodka when we had spare time. One night, I came home so late, early in the morning actually, that to my horror I bumped into my father as he was leaving for work. Again, my mother bravely ran interference, "Leave her alone. She's a college student and she knows what she's doing." Of course, I had no idea what I was doing. There was no role model for me. There were no role models for any of us who had no professional or educated women in our families.

Other kids I met, locals who had attended other high schools, taught me how to play cards. Every day after class ended, we gathered in the Student Center. I learned to play Hearts and became good enough at it to earn some cigarette and lunch money every day. Once I had enough money, I switched to playing Bridge for the day (not for money), a game which still brings me great joy, satisfaction, and frustration, mostly because I get upset with myself when I think I haven't played as well as I can. I feel just as competitive today as I did then, when my partner and I, like two hustlers, hit the duplicate bridge clubs, played against old, wealthy, suburban women whom we defeated regularly. Ironically, nowadays, it is the old-timers who defeat me.

I went to McGill University to get a college degree because that is what I needed to become a librarian; it coincided with my father's advice that I be independent; and it was the path to an MRS. degree. Shocking as that may be, I had no burning interest in any one subject and didn't like most of my classes. I didn't find many of them either intellectually stimulating or challenging. Truth be known, the only thing I learned at McGill was how to play Bridge. In one letter where Herm was trying to apologize for not coming during his winter break, he wrote, "Besides that you'd be in school all day, and even if I came with you, I'd probably end up watching you play cards…." It was true. All my time at McGill that year was spent either playing cards or planning some scheme that would enable me to make free long distance telephone calls to the U.S., or to go to school there.

Every time we separated, Herm and I felt extremely sad and had difficulty returning to a life that always felt like it was on hold. Surprisingly, or not for a 17-year-old girl, I was not feeling totally secure in our relationship. I always worried if a letter was late or if Herm didn't take every opportunity to come to Montreal to see me. I kept looking for ways to stay more connected. Telephone calls were expensive and unsatisfyingly short, and the cost of air travel was prohibitive.

I kept my promise to Herm and naively and secretly applied to Temple University. I was elated to be accepted for my second year, for the fall semester of 1968. Once again, I ran face-first into the brick wall of my parents' beliefs. In their view, a young girl did not leave her parents' home until marriage, ever. Even though that was not the plan, they would never in a thousand years approve, thinking we would be living together. There was much screaming and yelling, all on my part, to no avail. My father was immovable. My mother was silent. My last inept rebuttal was, "This is so old fashioned. There is no reason why I can't go to school in the States."

Sandu had the last word: "You are not leaving this house until you are married!"

My pride and sense of independence wounded, I sent Temple a letter saying that I would not be attending in the fall. Then, in a flash of inspiration it occurred to me that the time had come. I called Herm, "Oh Hermie, let's get married." I'd broken the ice! So I guess I was the one who proposed. And Herm immediately agreed.

Since I would have to continue at McGill for my second year, an American university would have to be postponed until junior year, after we were married. "Well," Herm wrote in his next letter, "I love you very much, & someday, one way or another, we won't have to write letters anymore," he assured me.

Chapter Thirteen

VALENTINE'S DAY

MASSACRE

IT IS HARD to re-capture the intensity of the teen anxiety I felt about Herm in the early years. I waited with trepidation for each letter or for the telephone to ring at an appointed time. I worried that Herm might break up with me without warning.

I was having fun in school but I was not very serious about my studies, nervously awaiting his every visit. At each such rendezvous, I had the same reaction I still have every time we are apart for more than a few days—butterflies in my stomach, heart rate up, and excited about catching sight of him. When I meet him at the bus station or airport, I can't wait to hold him, look up to meet his blue eyes and then, the lovely bear hug that sets the world right.

Things improved once we decided to get married after Herm's graduation from Temple, following my sophomore year. We hatched a plan for us to get engaged in the summer of 1968 and spend the summer together, working either in Montreal or Philadelphia. A wedding would take place the following year.

So as Valentine's Day 1968 approached, I was looking forward to Herm's card. I ran home from McGill, no bridge game or work schedule on that day, to check the mail. There, I found Herm's funny, twenty-five cent-card (can you imagine), which I quickly took to my room, barely stopping to say hello to Mamaia. Jumping onto my bed, I leaned against the pillows and headboard as I opened the card with relish.

I was shocked to find not only that Herm had written, in tiny script, all over the three sides of the 3.5" by 8" card, but another 8 pages, the longest letter he ever wrote. I did not know he was capable of such tiny script, though I realized later that his writing style depends on his mood. Something was up. Writing in miniature is his anxious writing style.

After a couple of introductory paragraphs, the letter took on a different tone. He wrote, "I don't really know what it is I am trying to say, and I don't know if I should even bring it up. But since it concerns us both, you at least should be aware of what I'm thinking—naturally I'm referring to our getting engaged. When I came back from Montreal it suddenly hit me like an explosion, how close we are to engagement." Oh no, a dagger to my heart!

All my anxieties flooded my brain. I tried to reconcile a Valentine's Day card expressing love with that sentence. I tried to make my way through the rest of his treatise, holding my breath. I read as quickly as possible, barely able to follow the letter. Where was all this coming from?

He said that I was a pretty, sweet, intelligent, nice girl he dearly loved; however, he sometimes saw another side to me that concerned him. This other self he found, "To be stern, unyielding, stubborn, much too proud, very unpliable, rarely lets herself be shown, very slow to forget grievances, lacks empathy, and very revenge-oriented." I felt deeply hurt and misjudged. But was it the truth or the misjudgment that brought me to my knees? I knew I was too proud to show weakness, very sensitive to criticism, but was always willing to help others, even generous to a fault. I also considered myself fair-minded, great in an argument and above all, persistent. At that point in my life, approaching 18, I had little understanding of what drove me. But I thought I understood what drove Herm—he wanted acceptance, to be liked, praise, attention, financial success.

I interpreted Herm's letter to mean that my very strengths were threatening him, making him feel powerless because he didn't know how to argue with me or feel comfortable doing it. Seeing anger in others was his Achilles' Heel. Anxiety poured out of him. There were times when I was angry but unable to express it. He had difficulty dealing with anger whether it was overtly or passively out there. He felt, "As if there was a real lack of basic understanding or communication between us," because I rarely verbalized my own sensitivities. He obviously was already on his way to becoming a psychologist. He thought, correctly, that I did not realize how much more sensitive to conflict he was than I. Conflict did not distress me as much because I grew up in a home with much more of it than Herm did in his home.

Even more problematic was his painful self-image as "A ridiculous, socially crippled fool," because of an embarrassing stuttering problem. I wondered where he was headed in his letter, but I knew and appreciated that he suffered great pain in some social situations. When we first met, I noticed that Herm stuttered at times although he rarely stuttered talking to me. However, when faced with a new situation, the fear of stuttering even more than the stuttering itself added an unnecessary stressor to his calm, easy personality. I was sensitive to his feelings, waiting patiently for him to recover his speech, as his groped about for a word.

While we grew up in very different families, our families had a lot in common, most important, our value systems. It was true that whereas his family was warm and communicative, mine labored with conflict and frequent confrontation. He said he sensed that no one liked my father, including me, but it was actually my mother who did not like him. My grandmother loved him and so did I.

My life's hardships had taught me to hide my emotions as a means of self-protection. Herm mixed up my being emotionally closed with my having too narrow a range of emotions, leaving him bewildered and frustrated. He felt he could only understand what I was feeling at the extremes, where I often was. Well, reading this letter left me confused—did he not like me?

He explained that he was unsure "If we would be good for each other, if we could live happily together for all those many years." Honestly, how does one discover that ultimate truth without being clairvoyant? "I suppose marriage, like the rest of life is sort of a gamble." Was I more of a risk-taker or did my need to be with him override my concerns? As a totally naive romantic, I never thought much past love—after all, does it not conquer all? I thought our relationship would develop effortlessly into one that would be the same as his parents'. What did I know about what a good marital relationship looked like?

As I continued reading I started to relax a little. Now I could take another breath. There was no mention of a break-up. He was just scared, sharing his fears, his limitations.

He asked me to take time and think through his heart-felt disclosures and respond gently, tactfully about what I was worried about in him. I did not take much time to think about my response, but instead, reacted quickly and emotionally. I didn't get really upset or worried about what he was saying. It seemed to me he was looking for reassurance. I began by explaining that our families thought and felt the same way about the important things such as marriage and education. I tried to counter some of his conclusions about me, just a little, because I didn't accept his characterizations of me as accurate. I told him I knew how much he struggled in social situations but more importantly, "We are both so young. We have so much growing up to do, together."

I also wrote that there was just no way that I was able to accurately assess all my own feelings. There were ideas I could not verbalize. Herm had told me a number of times how badly he had been affected by Lenny's break-up with his first wife. Herm had thought she was perfect, "She was beautiful, warm, funny and always fun." He was close to her. He could not understand what went wrong.

For the first time, I told Herm that I had always looked up to him. He had wonderful qualities like patience, consideration, a sense of humor and an ability to make me laugh. I thought these were not only vital to a successful marriage but also and a good counterbalance to me. Just as my boldness and proactive style balanced his shyness, passivity, and anxiety. Maybe it was an old fashioned idea about relationships, one person complementing the other. Maybe it was the marriage idealized on *I Love Lucy*. In every episode, chaos ensued because Lucy never listened to Ricky and Ricky always forgave Lucy her mistakes.

Realistically, I asked how much time had we spent together? Time when we could have discussed such in-depth feelings, thoughts, or concerns? We had seen each other maybe ten times and communicated almost exclusively in letters. This conversation was timely but difficult to do in letters written and received two weeks apart. Herm, however, was pleased and relieved with my response, writing "You showed tact & tenderness, & I was appreciative." The trauma of facing each other's feelings brought out important issues in our relationship and brought a new level of closeness. It cleared the air tremendously.

Neither one of us mentioned an engagement in the first letter that followed. However, a few weeks later, there was another surprise: Herm announced that he was coming to Montreal.

Another frenzy of activity began at home, my mother cleaning the house and preparing food. My father warning that I had to finish university before there was going to be any wedding. I just worried that everyone would get along. I didn't want to see any of the conflict my family was capable of. Up to then, my parents had always been on their best behavior with Herm.

In what turned out to be a family affair, again, Herm and his parents arrived on a Saturday afternoon in early spring for a beautiful weekend in Montreal. The next day found us all sitting in our crowded little living room. My father sat in the armchair in front of the large picture window all by himself, the patriarch presiding over his clan. It was just an illusion. He knew it, and the women of the household played along, as always.

Herm's parents sat on the couch perpendicular to the armchair with Herm perched on the end closest to my father. My mother and grandmother sat on folding chairs across from the couch, while I sat on my piano bench directly across from my father, on the opposite end of the room. There were refreshments on the coffee table: my mother's delicious marble cake, Turkish coffee, and a bottle of vodka. Someone was pretty optimistic.

With tension in the air, everyone sat quietly, expectantly. I must have been tongue-tied myself because I don't remember any preliminary chitchat. Herm looked like he was about to be taken to the guillotine, his face ashen with fear. He told me later, "I was nervous, feeling awkward and embarrassed." He said to my father, "As you know, Ann and I have been together for a couple of years. (I thought to myself, almost three years.) We love each other very much and we want to get married."

My father, with his very broad smile and a blush, said, "Sure. We like you and expect that you will make a good life for Ann. My main concern is that my daughter finish college." Yeah! I screamed in my head. The tension eased as everyone started to shake hands. Herm came and put his arm around me. We smiled at each other with great joy, no kissing allowed, but we were both very happy.

My mother started pouring coffee and serving cake. Sandu and Moishe started drinking shots of vodka. Herm had the good sense not to say anything about when we would get married. I knew there were many things left unsaid and realized it was better that way. He was showing wisdom beyond his years. I felt as though I was watching a movie unfold before me, about me, with me as only an observer. They were talking about me as if I had no say in the matter. Herm should have held my hand while he was talking to my father, but we were always afraid to show any affection in his presence. It never occurred to us to question why the proposal had included both sets of parents and a grandparent, as if we were 12 years old!

As they were drinking shots, Herm then pulled out a little jewelry box and with hands a bit shaky, put an engagement ring on my finger. It was a beautiful white gold branch-like setting that wrapped around my finger and ended in a pear shaped diamond. I loved the ring and showed it off to everyone in the room, smiling proudly. "Herm picked it out without me," I assured them. My grandmother was joyful that she would be alive to see my wedding.

Herm boasted that he had taken Sarita, Lenny's fiancée, with him to buy the ring but that he had chosen it himself. I decided then that he had great taste in jewelry. He felt that she would be able to validate his choice on my behalf since Sarita and I had become good friends. Sarita, who was in her mid-twenties, taught me how to put on make up and I taught her how to sew and bake. He knew that I looked up to her as much wiser because she had been part of the dating scene for a while. Herm and Lenny called us the two Communists because Sarita had come from Cuba a few years earlier and obviously, I was from Romania. Before the year was out, I traveled to Philadelphia for Lenny and Sarita's wedding.

I was relieved that everything had gone well. In my silent celebration, I was so happy I was ready to burst but knew I had to contain my joy. I could explode later. This was only the first step toward being together, so we had to tread lightly with our families. Both families were still resistant to a wedding before graduation ceremonies.

We finished the weekend with discussions about my going to Philadelphia for the summer and an official engagement party there. The Valentine's Day Massacre turned out to be a mere kerfuffle, but a necessary one. That made me happiest of all.

Chapter Fourteen

Mordy, Poland

IT WAS SO HARD to separate after such a short visit but it was such an exhilarating time. When a couple of months later I went back to Philadelphia, I was an engaged woman—ah, and how wonderful our first engaged kiss out of my parents' glare!

We took our first marvelous adventure together—a bus to New York for a special day in the city. We still look back on the day fondly because it led to so many later ones. We saw "Planet of the Apes" with Charlton Heston, yes, same guy as in *Ben Hur*. On the bus, we ate Pesche's prepared Passover lunch, hard boiled eggs and matzo brei (fried matzo) pancakes. We felt so grown up, having the freedom to go and do whatever our hearts desired and come back on our own schedule, really late, smooching in the last row of the bus all the way home.

About this time, Moishe and Pesche became concerned that the old Wynnefield neighborhood where they rented an apartment was irrevocably changing, as many of the Jewish families they knew began moving out. They stayed put until one day the upstairs tenant threw out her greasy wash-water over the railing right onto Pesche's fresh laundry. They decided it was time for them to carve out their piece of the American dream elsewhere.

They bought a pretty brick duplex, their first house, on small tree-lined Westwood Lane near the "Main Line," in Overbrook Hills, just across the City Line Avenue border of Philadelphia proper. It was close enough to walk along Haverford Avenue to a synagogue in Overbook Park. The house had everything they wanted: three bedrooms and two bathrooms, a finished paneled basement where Moishe could pay his bills at his "new" desk, a covered front porch, and a garage. The garage, which was never used for that purpose, served as a storage and workshop area. Closing was scheduled for May of 1968, which made the summer an opportune time for me to spend with them. Herm wrote, "Just to show you how much my folks are counting on you to come, we're including you in our reckonings of who to put in which rooms." But Overbrook Hills was such a long, long way from where they started.

Poland, which was caught in a tug of war between Prussia (Germany) and Russia for more than 200 years by the start of World War II, had had a large Jewish population since the 14th century; its King Kzimicrz II protected the Jewish community from persecution and the population flourished. In the late 18th century, four million Jews from the former Polish/Lithuanian state came under Russian rule. Czarina Catherine the Second banished Jewish merchants out of the cities into small villages called "shtetls" in the countryside, known as the Pale of Settlement. By the 19th century, several insurrections led to fewer restrictions but shtetl life continued. Mordy was one such shtetl, little more than a stop on the train line between Warsaw and the East.

Each shtetl had at its core a small, dirt-poor Jewish community, surrounded by Polish-owned farms. Robbed of their livelihood, Jews generally turned to trades such as tailoring, shoe repair and commerce, trading goods and services with other locals, and living peacefully most of the time. These hard-working, honorable, and religious people had become resigned to the terrifying pogroms, which were as common as inevitable.

According to Pesche, "Where we lived, violence was perpetrated by soldiers, renegades or outsiders, not by our neighbors. The children all played together and the Polish community left us alone until the war brought the Germans and Russians. When Germans and Russians moved in, they ruined it."

Pesche was born in Sarnaki, Poland in either 1910 or 1911. Sarnaki was a shtetl about 100 miles east of Warsaw, not far from Mizrich (Międzyrzec), a larger community. She was a cheerful, bright, outgoing woman, with dark brown hair and blue eyes that she passed on to her children. She loved to sing and dance, but had a serious side, too. Her father made his living buying and selling hay and corn. He was also a moneylender, lending to "poor" people. As the youngest of seven siblings whose mother died when she was only two years old, she was raised by her oldest, much older, sister, Leah. "I did not like living with my beautiful sister because my cousins were grown. I had no one to go to school with."

Embarrassed about her lack of education, Pesche often lamented not going past the 3rd grade. It is a shame she felt bad about herself because she was street smart and clever, qualities that later saved her and her family's lives.

After a few years with Leah, Pesche returned to live with her father until the age of seventeen when, like many other young women, she went to work in one of Warsaw's abundant dry-goods factories. During the 1920s and 1930s a majority of the Jewish population in Warsaw was employed in the manufacture of clothing. Pesche joined the ranks of sweater-knitters, young women who were the backbone of the factories.

A soft smile lightened her face when she told me, "I was going out with young men. We went together to the Zionist meetings. We all planned to move to Israel as soon as possible. One such young man was a shoemaker, Mottel, I think his name was, who wanted to marry me. He followed me like a shadow, but I couldn't stand him. A shoemaker? Where do I come to a shoemaker? No!"

I was surprised by the independence she enjoyed. She was happy in Warsaw. Her only obligation was to send money home from her job, until after a few years, she had to return home to care for her aging father.

Pesche was in her eighties by the time she told me her story. By then, she could only remember two brothers: one whose name she could no longer remember who died young serving in the Polish army, and Binyumin who was much older than she. Binyumin lived with his wife and children in the little shtetl of Mordy. Pesche also had four sisters, two of whom still lived in Mordy then. There was such a large age difference between the siblings that Binyumin was a father figure in her stories. Shabbat and other holidays were spent at his table where he presided over the family.

Pesche met Moishe in Mordy, where he was born and where he and his mother operated a dry goods store on the square. "My father had died by then," Moishe told me. Like Pesche, Moishe had much older brothers whose children were Moishe's age or older. One brother and sister remained in Mordy.

Moishe approached Pesche at the Mordy train stop when she was returning from one of her trips to visit her family who had remained in Sarnaki. "I recognized her from the feed shop," he told us. "Pesche would come into the store with her sister-in-law."

"Moishe threw away all his friends and he went around with me," Pesche lovingly recalled sixty years later. They courted for four years before they decided to marry. Knowing Pesche's family's fine reputation, Moishe treated her very well. "My father had been a rabbi and collected interest on loans." They went to her brother Binyumin who substituted for her late father, for approval.

Moishe and Pesche were married in the mid 1930s, the exact date lost to us as is any wedding photograph. Lenny was born in 1938, and named after Pesche's late father, Label.

Moishe and Pesche in Poland, shortly after their wedding.

"When war broke out in Europe in 1939," Pesche told me, "we were living in Mizrich. Moishe was working as a furrier." Mizrich had an organized Jewish population and was a community larger than any of the numerous shtetls. It flourished because it had developed a unique industry of producing and distributing its world famous hog-hair brushes which allowed its population financial independence. It also had a second lucrative industry in fur. Like Galati, since before the turn of the century, Mizrich had been a hotbed of Zionism to which young people were drawn from the shtetl.

A gentle and unassuming man who preferred play to work, Moishe was an unlikely soldier. However, when the Polish military came to Mizrich to round up men for their force, he had no choice but to go, leaving his wife and baby behind.

Wars came and went but this war was different. As Pesche described it, "This was not about conquering territory but about killing people." Alone with her infant son, Pesche made her way back to Mordy to find her brother and sisters. With all able-bodied men conscripted, the women and children left behind were forced to fend for themselves.

After its quick defeat, the Polish army was disbanded and many men did make their way back slowly to the shtetls. News of loved ones was hard to get and unreliable. Word of mouth was the only form of communication. There was no reliable transportation. The German trains were dangerous because they were being used to transport Jews to concentration camps.

In Mordy, as in many other shtetls, there was little food, no news about husbands, fathers, or sons; a dark cloud of fear cast a long shadow over everyone. Pesche lived with her sisters and their children for a few months until rumors began circulating that the Germans, headed toward Mordy were killing all Jewish babies as they marched east. Pesche still believed this to be true when she told the story 50 years later, and was very graphic in her descriptions; "They took the children by their legs and swung them like chickens and smashed their heads against a wall." Horrified, she quickly realized that, unlike her sisters who had ties and homes in the village, she had nothing to lose by fleeing. "I was not going to sit and wait for death," she explained. And so she left her siblings, despite their protestations.

Miraculously, Moishe, who had suffered a gunshot wound to his knee, did make his way back, walking for weeks, stopping at hospitals occasionally for food. As a wounded soldier he was entitled to food. Ironically, other soldiers who were uninjured were not so lucky.

Frightened and cut off from family, Pesche had nothing to rely on but her sharp wits. She went to one of her late father's debtors who was still making weekly payments on a debt. In exchange for forgiveness of one's month's payment, he agreed to ferry her across the Bug River, which formed the new border between Poland and Russia.

Driven by an extreme sense of resolve and buoyed by occasional messages passed on from person to person that Moishe was on his way back, she could not and would not leave the area. "I hoped that soon Moishe would return and everything would be over."

Pesche planned to follow her sister Leah who had already crossed the border into Russia and to leave Lenny with her so she could be free to return to Poland to wait for Moishe. She would go back to retrieve him. To get ready for the crossing, she packed a sack filled with a large supply of farfel (dried dough) and some bedding in a large tub. It turned out that the tub was larger than the boat so their things had to be unpacked straight into the boat, including the tub she needed to bathe the baby. As the oars scraped the bottom of the river with each stroke, she and the oarsman thought they would be discovered by Russian sentries and mistaken for spies. However, the trip was uneventful except for one Russian they bribed once on land who then followed them to Leah's house to make sure they were telling the truth.

The next day, she and Lenny joined an army of refugees. Recalling that day, Pesche elaborated, "I knew the refugees were running back and forth across the Russian border. I figured that if we kept moving, we would be safe." Leaving Mordy, with no place to go, was a brave and remarkably prescient choice. It was the last time Pesche saw any of her immediate family.

For the next several months, Pesche and the other refugees who went east with her, managed to stay alive in the thick forests on the banks of the Bug River, inside the Russian border. When rumors reached them that the Russians were advancing west, they made their way back to Poland, sleeping on the ground at the border until authorities opened the crossing.

The refugees learned their way through the forest, mastering how to avoid being swallowed by the swamps, marshes, and decayed wood. "In the forest, we collected and ate blueberries and mushrooms," remembered Pesche. "But, it was a dangerous place. One man who lost his way in the forest began screaming for help. The others tried to find him by following the screams, but by the time they found him the next day, he was dead."

Pesche was unwilling to discuss all the details about her war years until she was in her eighties and was already showing the ravages of Alzheimer's disease. Moishe "came exactly the day that I had to leave." Her saga of what she went through alone and what they went through together became entangled, but one story, memorialized on videotape, still brings me to tears. She tells of how they sometimes escaped from place to place by hopping on the trains that regularly made their way through the Polish/Russian battle zone. In one instance, the train was moving slowly, so Moishe was able to climb on the train. However, Pesche who had a bandaged leg and was carrying Lenny, couldn't climb up after him or keep up with the moving train. In panicked desperation, she threw the child up to Moishe as she walked on, the train leaving her behind. How they managed to find each other once again remains a mystery.

After the Russians and Germans signed a non-aggression pact in 1939, dividing Poland between themselves, approximately 250,000 Jewish immigrants were allowed across the Bug River into Russia. Many were transported to Siberian work camps. Although conditions in the camps were very harsh, those Jews who survived in Siberia were spared deportation to concentration camps.

Pesche explained that they had refused Russian passports so they had to stay one step ahead of the Russians to avoid transport. Eventually, inexplicably, Pesche, Moishe, and Lenny were among those who decided once again, to cross the Bug River, which was near to where they were living in eastern Poland before they, too, were transported to Siberia, "a real hell." Food was rationed; for instance, for a child, they allowed five grams of bread and half a glass of milk. Moishe who did not want to do manual labor (he preferred bartering), was forced by the Russian authorities to cut down trees, as was Pesche. As Pesche told it, "We did what we had to do." In return for labor, they received "a piece of bread and a glass of milk." They also bartered for food using shirts and underwear rescued from dead soldiers, which they bleached and sewed into other clothing items. They bartered cigarettes for bread. There was no bedding except for a small bed fashioned out of straw for Lenny.

On one occasion, Moishe was imprisoned by the Russians as punishment for black market "hondling"—that is, selling goods without a permit. He spent a couple of months in jail before Pesche was able to bribe the jailers to buy his freedom.

Some of Moishe's siblings' children had left for the United States and Israel in the 1920s and 30s and were spared likely annihilation in Europe. Moishe's one remaining brother and sister were not so lucky. They were just two of three million Jews who were exterminated in Poland alone, half the total number of European Jews during the War—not in or from combat, but by plan of the Nazi regime. Those murdered represented 90 per cent of Poland's Jews. Records show that most of those Jewish refugees who surrendered or were caught in Eastern Poland were immediately transported to the Belzec or Treblinka extermination camps. It is a staggering number of people to come from one country and could not have happened without the help of much of the local population. It is nothing short of a miracle, not just remarkable luck and ingenuity, that Pesche, Moishe, and Lenny survived as had others who chose to flee rather than surrender.

It was extremely painful for Pesche to recount the losses but I think she felt it was necessary to keep the memories of those who were gone. It was equally hard for me to listen without getting upset about the unspeakable evil that was done, while marveling at their inner strength and resilience. Re-telling the tale always brings tears to my eyes. Through those chats with Moishe and Pesche I learned to speak Yiddish, interrupting to ask about an unfamiliar word. Although Pesche spoke a passable though fractured English, when talking about old times she reverted to Yiddish.

Amid the stories of horror, Pesche was overjoyed to learn after the war that one of her nephews, Binyumin's son, Shimon, survived the war. I met Shimon and his wife when they visited Philadelphia from Buenos Aires in 1967.

Shimon and I hit it off and he was very eager to share his story. He told me, "I and a few other young men escaped from a concentration camp somewhere around 1943 and hid out in the countryside, moving from farm to farm where we stole food and lived in underground tunnels. One day, I was accidentally discovered by a Polish farmer who was going to expose me. I had no choice but to kill him with my bare hands in order to save myself. Another more tolerant and kind farmer hid me in an underground bunker for the remainder of the war. It must have been another year. Every few days he would bring some food and news."

Shimon survived the war, then made his way through Italy and various other places, until he found a haven in Buenos Aires, Argentina, where he lived to a ripe old age. There, he continued to reap the rewards of perseverance and hard work through his children, many grandchildren and great-grandchildren until 2012 when he passed away, already in his nineties.

Chapter Fifteen

NEU FREIMANN, MUNICH

AS THE WAR came to an end in 1945, more than 11 million refugees were freed by the Allies from concentration camps, labor camps, and prisoner-of-war camps. Added to them were millions more who ran in terror from the advancing Russian Army because of rumors of rape, looting, and murder. At first, most of the displaced persons' needs were provided by the Allied forces. Eventually, it was the United Nations Refugee Assistance Committee (UNRAC) that arranged for the refugees to be either returned to their native country or to be temporarily settled in Displaced Persons (DP) Camps all over Europe. Moishe, Pesche, and Lenny joined their ranks when they left Siberia, choosing not to become Russian citizens.

Initially, Moishe's family rode another train back to Poland to find extended family, expecting survivors. They could find not a single family member still alive in Mordy, nor evidence that Jews had lived there. No graves, gravestones or cemeteries. There were no other Jews. As in Mordy, Mizrich's (where Pesche's family lived during the war) Jewish population was totally annihilated. All its Jews murdered. Unwilling to remain among people, some of whom hated them enough to kill them, Moishe and Pesche agreed to be re-settled in an American-run DP camp, Neu Freimann, located in the outskirts of Munich, Germany. This had been an already existing planned community for workers, turned into a self-sustaining encampment by the US Army. A chain link fence was installed to separate its inhabitants from the German population.

The planned community was originally built in 1934 by the Bavarian Motor Works (BMW) workers who were part of the growing war machine. They were engineers, carpenters, plumbers, and electricians who knew they were building their own future homes. When construction was completed, each of the workers was permitted a house chosen by lottery.

The American Army, under the auspices of the UNRAC, took over the community, evicting its German residents. Thousands of refugees, mostly Jews, arriving in successive waves took their place.

One of the original homes in the Displaced Persons Camp.

The development scheme consisted of small, identical and neatly designed homes, arranged on a U-shape grid of streets, surrounding a communal park area. Each small house was one and one-half stories high with a sloped roof, making up a main room, kitchen, and bathroom on the first floor and two rooms on the second floor. It was situated on a small plot of land, surrounded by a white picket fence. A small vegetable garden sprung up on each plot. Two families were assigned to share each home including the bathroom and kitchen. For those who had endured horrifying living conditions in the forests of Poland and cramped concrete Russian bunkers, these were luxury accommodations.

Years later after they had left the DP camp, we learned that Pesche and Moishe shared their home for a time with the parents of one of our closest friends, Manya. Manya's parents, Michael and Deborah, who settled in New York, asked Moishe and Pesche to look after their daughter when she started to study at Temple University in Philadelphia years later. Herm met her at the end of the summer of 1965, when Manya came to visit him in Atlantic City. Moishe and Pesche, apparently wishing to get me off Herm's mind, thought it would be a good idea to take Manya with them on their bi-weekly trip "down the shore." I met her a few months later. We have been dear friends ever since.

We learned more about conditions in the DP camp from Deborah, then in her nineties, another feisty and strong-willed woman who survived indescribable conditions by her remarkable wits. Still too wary to share many details 65 years after the end of the war, she reluctantly revealed to us that she and Pesche did not get along in the camp.

According to Deborah, there was constant friction with Pesche because she insisted on keeping a kosher kitchen, which Deborah did not want to do. Still smarting after all this time, she told us, "I had to wait every day until Pesche was done with the kitchen before she would let me use it." Besides, Deborah told us, they also competed in "business," each trying to eke out a living selling "shmatas" (rags and clothes).

I learned from another DP camp survivor, Sammy, whom I met only recently, that he was placed in one of the many camps in Berlin. He was a teenager at the time. While in the camp, there was much bitter fighting between families such as his and those recognized in the camp as having aided the Nazis in the concentration camps. Their excuses or explanations did not help them. Camp administrators had to re-locate these targets of wrath to other camps.

Residents of the DP camps understood these were temporary quarters. They had no way to know how long their stay would be or where they would be going next. Despite being emotionally and physically scarred and battered by a war with plans specifically aimed at their annihilation and which left them dispersed without families and resources, they had children who desperately needed their care and attention. Thus, they went about the business of restoring a semblance of normalcy to their lives, using their skills at coping with uncertainty.

At the Displaced Persons Camp in 1946. Lenny was eight years old.

Incident after incident, atrocity after atrocity, I never cease to marvel at how resilient the human spirit is. Like water finding its stable level, people look for a way to restore a normal life.

An economy sprung up with mundane, everyday endeavors. The refugees started small businesses, bartering and trading with each other. Quickly, community institutions sprung up on the streets bordering on the park, including a kosher butcher shop, a small school, an orchestra, and of course, a synagogue.

Men and boys of all ages, including Lenny who was now seven or eight years old, entertained themselves playing soccer on the grassy, large lawn of the central park area. In one of the few historical films of the time, there is one of General Eisenhower touring the Neu Freimann DP camp in 1949, shortly before the last of its residents were re-settled and the American Army allowed the original occupants to return. The grainy film shows some of the community buildings but highlights the soccer game in which Manya swears she can see a vibrant young man, her father.

Life went on. They worked. They married. They bore children. Pesche lost a baby girl to a miscarriage but Herm was born in 1947, in the bathroom of the house on Spitzer Strasse in Neu Freimann or so family legend has it. Whatever else they were, the Germans were superb record keepers, and Herm was finally able to get a birth certificate from the City of Munich in 2011.

A tender moment in the Camp, Lenny holding infant Herm.

Chapter Sixteen

PHILADELPHIA

IT HAD LONG been Pesche's wish to go to Palestine. She'd been an active member of a Zionist organization in her youth in Poland, and she and Moishe were planning to immigrate when the Holocaust intervened. After the War, they still wanted to go to Palestine and as "displaced persons" requested re-settlement there. But, few countries opened their arms to Jewish refugees, and British-occupied Palestine was not one of them.

Great Britain had long had an ambivalent relationship with the Jews. When the Ottoman Empire was divided at the end of World War I, Palestine fell under British control. In 1917, a letter written by Britain's Foreign Secretary, Arthur James Balfour to prominent Zionist Baron de Rothschild, known as the Balfour Declaration, recognized the rights of the Jewish people to a land of their own. It was followed by Churchill's White Paper of 1922, which continued to support the immigration of Jews to Palestine.

However, in 1939, the fate of millions of Jews was sealed by then British Colonial Secretary MacDonald's White Paper. It limited annual immigration to Palestine to 75,000, and prohibited further land purchases by Jews. MacDonald was motivated by a desire to maintain a stable proportion of Arabs and Jews in Palestine. But as a consequence, Jewish immigration was greatly curtailed at a time when millions desperately needed a safe haven. The State of Israel, as a land where Jews could go freely, would not be recognized by the United Nations until 1948.

Thus, the doors to Palestine were closed to millions of Jewish refugees except for the seventy thousand who were smuggled in by underground militant groups, the Haganah, Irgun, and Lehi. Their struggle was publicized by humanitarian Ruth Gruber, a journalist for the New York Herald Tribune. She would eventually write *Destination Palestine, the Struggle of 1947*. At the age of 101, she recalled the details of that difficult struggle, vividly and articulately as I listened spellbound, at New York's Museum of Jewish Heritage. Gruber died in 2016 during the writing of her book, at the age of 105.

In 1958, *Exodus,* the best selling novel by Leon Uris, widened public awareness of the struggle. In Montreal, we saw the 1960 epic movie based on the book, shortly after we arrived. The actors wore the same clothes I'd worn and sang the same songs in a landscape I remembered so well. Hearing the national anthem, *Hatikvah*, at the end of the movie still brings tears to my eyes.

The Hubers on the trip to America in 1949.

Those displaced persons not permitted to go to Palestine, or who did not wish to go there, had to find relatives in other countries like Canada, Australia, England, or the United States, to sponsor their immigration. Those with no family or sponsorship went to countries with more liberal immigration policies, including Argentina, Brazil, and Chile.

Finally, four long years after their arrival at the DP camp, Moishe and Pesche's turn came. Pesche, Moishe, Lenny, and two-year-old Herm were permitted to travel to the United States. While America was not their first choice, its rumored streets paved with gold had an appeal.

Herm and Len just before sailing to America.

The family's immigration was sponsored by Moishe's paternal cousin, Dora, about 20 years his senior. She had immigrated to Philadelphia in 1920 to join her husband, Jacob, who'd preceded her. Moishe and Dora had not maintained contact after Dora's departure from Poland, but the United States Refugee Relocation Assistance Committee located the family in the United States. Co-operating with the American Joint Distribution Committee and the National Council of Jewish Women, the agency spent a year working with Dora and Jacob on the Huber family's immigration.

After a long anticipated departure, the family traveled to the United States by boat from Bremen, making their way on the USAT Mercy to the port of New York. They arrived on June 19, 1949, with five pieces of luggage, having lost an unmarked wooden crate of clothing because they did not have the twelve cents to properly arrange for the baggage. The wandering souls made their way by train from New York to Philadelphia. Lenny, then 11 years old remembers that, "Someone picked us up in a 1948 black Buick sedan at the 30th Street Station." It was the biggest automobile any of them had ever seen.

Dora, Moishe's cousin, and her husband, Jacob in 1947. The baby at the bottom is their grandson, David.

Dora and Jacob generously put their cousins up for two weeks in their home at 53rd and Locust Street before Moishe and Pesche found their own apartment nearby, at Ruby and Market Streets, and then a job. Quickly and resourcefully, they started to fend for themselves with only a few words of English between them.[2]

The Hubers at their first apartment in Philadelphia, 1955.

Somehow, with ingenuity and courage that still amazes me, Pesche and Moishe managed to lease a hot dog stand from an enterprising 22-year-old named Bob Rasmussen, who had the rights to the concession stand in Strawberry Mansion, a north Philadelphia neighborhood that took its name from a 19th century restaurant that had served strawberries and cream to some of Philadelphia's wealthiest inhabitants.

_____

2. Dora and Moishe's families lost contact several years after they moved out. It was not until 60 years later, and only by happenstance, that Lenny met Dora's grandson, David. David was quite excited to finally hear from the two boys he was never able to identify in an old family photograph: Lenny and Herm as young children.

Pesche selling hot dogs in Memorial Hall
in Philadelphia's Fairmount Park.

The whole Huber family became involved in the vending
enterprise. As his parents manned the hot dog stand, Lenny trolled
with an ice cream wagon. However, in the fall, he was enrolled in
the sixth grade in a public school, the Huey School, where he soon
mastered English without an accent.

Later, with preschooler Herm by her side, Pesche operated
Rasmussen's hot dog stand in Fairmount Park, on the banks of the
Schuylkill River, one of the largest urban parks in the world. One
Saturday morning during our courtship, Pesche told me an endearing
story of how gullible Herm was at such a tender age, although I think
he still is (at not so tender an age). "This man approached me and was
about to rob me. So, I whispered to Chaim (Herm) in Yiddish to go
get a policeman, but when the robber asked, 'What did she say?' What
do you think Chaim did?" she asked.

"Chaim obligingly translated for the robber, 'She told me to call
the police.'" Even as little more than a toddler, he always tried to
please. Pesche blew a small red whistle hanging from a string around
her neck, to alert police and the robber ran away.

Meanwhile, like Sandu, Moishe got a job in a factory, a millinery plant, and he complained about the job just as regularly and bitterly. He laughed at himself when he'd told me how much he disliked the factory work and its rigid rules and schedule. At one point, he'd hoped the factory would burn down. Mostly, I think these proud young men who had survived such hardships found it hard to take orders from a boss.

Eventually, Moishe's factory job led to a venture with their former housemates at the DP camp. Moishe and Michael began operating a hot dog vending business in New York's Yankee Stadium, selling all-beef Nathan's hot dogs. Both were short men with heavy accents and aquiline noses. There must have been some funny stories from this immigrant alliance in a quintessentially American setting, but alas, they have been lost.

The hot dog business, in turn, led to a series of more secure and respectable businesses for Moishe. There was a dry goods store where he sold shmatas, followed by a grocery store on the corner of 16th Street and Allegheny with other former housemates from the DP camp. Unfortunately, they had a falling out, lending support for the truism that, "One should never go into business with friends."

Around 1957, two remarkable events shaped the rest of Moishe's and Pesche's lives: First, the family moved to the apartment on Euclid Avenue near City Line and 54th Street. Pesche gave up the hot dog stand and upgraded to her own storefront near Euclid Avenue, selling eggs the family bought at the farms in Vineland, New Jersey. On the sidewalk outside the storefront, Herm sat in the hot sun frying ants with a magnifying glass, apparently in preparation for frog dissection in high school.

Second, Moishe met Meyer, also a refugee, and the two men began a long-term partnership operating Harry's Market. Their wives also worked in the store. The partners must have purchased it from Harry because neither was named Harry.

Florence with Moishe, Pesche, and Lenny.
She and her family lived on the second floor.

When they moved to Euclid venue, their upstairs neighbors were a newlywed couple, Florence and Charlie, also Holocaust survivors. Charlie had been Lenny's friend. It was Lenny who suggested the apartment when the couple was married. Pesche referred to Florence as her daughter and Lenny thought of her as his sister. By the time we met, my future in-laws and Charlie and Florence had grown quite close, almost like parents and children.

When my mother and I met them in 1965, they had two small children, "Little" Lenny and Robin. Herm was their steady babysitter. He actually taught me how to put on a diaper when it was our turn to have a child years later. Truth be told, I still had to hold an instruction manual in one hand, while I changed my first child's first diaper with the other. (Everyone had left me home with the baby while they went shopping for all our basic needs. No preparation had been made prior to her birth in deference to Jewish superstition.)

Florence, who otherwise was quite shy, was warm, funny and gentle once she got to know you. She was tall and quite large for a woman, with an impish smile, always ready for a joke. When she hugged you, it was truly a bear hug. We laughed hysterically, many times, when we relived times we spent together, including an incident early in our courtship, when we went to visit Crystal Cave, Pennsylvania. The cave walls were made of crystals, the formations known as stalagmites and stalactites, a fascinating experience although a cold one.

Around lunchtime at the site, Florence was hungry but afraid to eat any non-kosher food in front of Herm, who she thought still kept scrupulously kosher. Little did she know how little he cared about keeping kosher, although he respected his parents' rules until he married and moved away from home. When Herm went to the restroom, Florence sprang into action and whispered to me, "Shhhhh!"

Then, she sprinted over to the hot dog stand, bought one and started to eat it as fast as she could, keeping a look out for Herm. When she saw him coming back sooner than expected, Florence quickly shoved the rest of it into her mouth, like those Coney Island hot-dog eating contestants, laughing all the time.

After my mother and I met them, we became life-long friends. Sadly, Charlie died at a young age and Florence moved to Florida. Years later, my mother and I loved visiting her whenever we traveled south to escape the harsh northern winters.

Florence lived until her mid-seventies. She had been traumatized by her war experiences, having been born in 1940, and only told us how her family escaped the Holocaust the year before she died. It was the last time we saw her. She showed us a book, *Fighting Back* by Harold Werner, a relative of hers who had written a memoir of his heroic experiences as a resistance fighter during the war in Poland. In it, there is a picture of 6-year-old Florence, shoeless in a shapeless frock, standing next to her parents, with a caption reading:

Zindel and Betty Honigman with their daughter Fella [Florence] in eastern Poland shortly after liberation in late summer 1944. Zindel escaped from a work detail at the Sobibor death camp together with two other camp inmates, by killing two guards and slipping away in the woods. On a moving train bound for Sobibor, Betty pushed her four-year-old daughter through a crack in the cattle car, then followed her and was hidden by friendly farmers in Gorzkow until Liberation. (Columbia University Press, 1992)

Florence's remarkable spirit was what shone through when we met and was the same spirit we observed in Moishe and Pesche. In retrospect, it was the same spirit my parents had.

Chapter Seventeen

HARRY'S MARKET

HARRY'S MARKET was a small grocery store and deli, the equivalent of today's bodega. Located in Powelton Village, a once elegant and affluent neighborhood in central Philadelphia, it was by the mid 1950s home to students from Drexel Institute of Technology, (affectionately referred to as Dreck Tech), and the University of Pennsylvania, as well as the homeless and the unemployed.

Harry's Market, with neatly lined shelving filled with an amazing array of grocery items, occupied a small space, a few steps down from street level on the side of a large, previously grand building complex that took up an entire block.

The small store even boasted a butcher section and a fresh fruit and vegetable section. When we got married, Moishe insisted that we stock our first apartment with all our basic needs from the store. Also, on every visit to us, they brought bags of groceries for their undoubtedly malnourished children. For years, I owned and used the classic broom, dustpan and pail from Harry's Market. I wish I'd held onto them as mementos.

Moishe at the register in Harry's Market.

Pesche usually manned the cash register near the front door while Moishe stocked the shelves and his partner manned the butcher shop. The neighborhood fell upon hard times and they were robbed several times in the late 1950s and 60s, once even at gunpoint. The way Moishe remembered it, "Five men with shotguns entered the store and made me and Meyer and everyone in the store lie down in the back room. They took all the cash, cigarettes and some food before they left. Everyone thought they were going to be killed." Having survived the Holocaust, Moishe did not appear to be traumatized by a mere robbery.

Whenever Herm and I visited the bustling market, we each helped to manage the cash register, separately. We learned to greet the customers while also keeping an eye on known shoplifters. The wall behind the counter was stacked full from ceiling to floor with merchandise and particularly, cigarettes, as one of the more expensive and popular commodities in the store.

Harry's Market made it possible for Moishe and Pesche to build a new life, to develop friendships with other "greener" (newcomers)— immigrants who were survivors and newcomers such as they were— to live more comfortably and to educate their children. Lenny, who was nine years older, attended high school at the highly regarded Akiba Hebrew Academy, which counts among its alumni a number of luminaries, including Mitch Albom, author of *Tuesdays with Morrie*.

Herm also attended Jewish parochial schools after a brief public school stint, starting with Beth Jacob, an orthodox grade school where children wore "payos" (very long sideburns) and religious garb; later, he also attended Akiba Hebrew Academy in Lower Merion. His graduating class only had twenty-three students but they all got an excellent education. Most of the students attended not only college, but went on to graduate education as well.

Pesche and Moishe placed such value on education that they made the sacrifice to pay, and even Akiba's reduced tuition was a struggle for them. Yet, they often lamented, "We paid $500 for every Hebrew word Herm learned, of which fortunately, there were not many."

It was also Harry's Market that eventually made it possible for them to realize the American dream, their own home in Overbrook Hills, a suburb near the Main Line in Philadelphia. The night before the closing, Moishe spent a sleepless night panicked about the $20,000 mortgage. He need not have worried. They made all the payments, regularly and on time including the last payment, made with much fanfare by Pesche in 1988.

Harry's Market was hard work, twelve hours a day on their feet, seven days a week but they continued to work there for many years until Moishe's death and Pesche's retirement about a decade later. When Pesche retired, the local residents warmly presented her with a fancy Certificate of Appreciation.

Chapter Eighteen

An Engagement Party

I ARRIVED a few weeks after their closing on the home. Herm's parents were so welcoming that they renovated the kitchen in its original footprint, leaving a tiny adjoining room to be a guest room for me. It had little more room than for a single bed, but I loved it because it was sunny and bright. It remained "Chanala's room" for years to come.

I met my in-laws at such a young age that they became an important influence in my life and we became very close. They were warm, loving and so generous it was impossible not to love them. Moishe was balding, with gray hair, blue eyes and was of medium height. He loved to tell funny stories and jokes. Pesche was very giving and enjoyed chatting, especially on Shabbat mornings, when she would often reminisce about her past.

Over the summer, Pesche and I worked at decorating the rest of the house together and preparing for a for Labor Day weekend engagement party. Pesche wanted my advice about the latest home fashions, a subject I knew nothing about; I was not really much help, but it was fun to go shopping together and discuss various styles and colors. And of course we discussed and made menu selections for our engagement party. It would all be homemade food, much of which would be prepared by Pesche since my cooking was basic, at best. We decided she'd make kreplach, similar to Italian tortellini or small Chinese dumplings. She was a marvel as she formed these delicacies effortlessly at amazing speed. I enjoyed her maternal company as she taught me to speak Yiddish. She would correct me whenever I used a wrong word, laughing very gently. Later in the day, she would report on my progress, including my mistakes, for the others to enjoy.

Pesche could be unintentionally funny. Her orthodox Jewish upbringing served to breed wariness of non-Jews and a rather small and limited view of the world. For example, one of Herm's Irish Catholic friends, Frank, once had a light-hearted discussion about religion with her. She began informing Frank that there are "Two religions in the world, right?"

"Oh, really?" was his surprised response.

"Yes," she asserted, "Jewish and non-Jewish," to which he chuckled.

Pesche was so easy to be with that we had a wonderful stress-free relationship, utterly unlike my relationship with my mother. My mother was often anxious, and at times overly critical. She was not so generous with her feelings, her time or her money. Regarding money, of course, Herm's parents had reached a point where they were much more financially secure than my family was. My mother always tried to be the parent and would never let her guard down. She was ever vigilant about my relationship with Herm, continuing to run interference between my father and me. My father, on the other hand, had been easier to be with when I was younger, especially when he took care of me while my mother worked. But, the older I got, the less comfortable he seemed to feel in my presence. He was shy and so easily embarrassed about anything feminine and personal. By my mid-teens, we stopped taking our long walks or having our talks.

Our limited interior design skills resulted in anchor-blue wall-to wall carpeting, a shag in true sixties fashion on which our children would later repeatedly slide down the stairs, as Pesche complained that they were wearing down the rug. Pesche also picked out a blue and gold cut-velvet couch with matching gold armchair, both of which she encased in industrial strength plastic. Our skin stuck to it every time we sat down, just about tearing our butts off when we got up. The only item on which she was willing to be a little more adventuresome was a side table with a shellac, shell top. Passé now, but quite daring then. I can't say that any of the furniture was really my style, since I did not yet have a style, but I think it was all in good taste and sturdy. It outlasted the childhoods of five grandkids over the next twenty years. Not only did manufacturers know how to make good quality furniture in those days, but people knew how to take care of their things. Of course, the plastic helped too.

During his college years, Herm always took a summer job to save money for his own expenses. One year he worked for the Post Office, picking up mail from myriad street-corner boxes. As we drove around the city, Herm proudly and assuredly pointed out each and every mailbox he had serviced. (He still does this.) The following year, when he couldn't find a summer job, he decided to attend summer school and help out in Harry's Market as "chief stock boy for $1.40 per hour." Herm's summer job the next year was in a tobacco warehouse, packing up cartons of cigarettes from which he reeked at the end of the day.

The summer we spent together at his parents' house allowed us every evening to compare notes about our day (something we still do). I told him about our designing and shopping experiences. He told us about the warehouse job, where he met all sorts of interesting blue-collar workers who treated him well. Most importantly, we managed to find concentrated periods of time to try out being together for more than a week at a time. Not only did we get along really well, but we loved being together. It was such a comfortable summer. I already felt a part of the Huber family. His parents seemed to feel comfortable with having me there, too. I often saw them warm toward one another.

They were also quite playful and frequently I would catch Moishe reaching around Pesche to plant a juicy kiss on her cheek, as she laughingly shooed him away.

The summer was not conflict-free, though, because there were arguments between Herm and his parents about the timing of our wedding. While my parents would have preferred for me to finish college first, as time passed, I think they were very happy to marry me off. Herm's parents worried that if we got married, he would forego an advanced degree as Lenny had. Their initial panic when I'd first appeared in Herm's life, which they worked through just before he started college, now reared its head again. We assured them we had a workable plan. I soothed them when I promised I would make sure he graduated. They eventually relented.

My parents and grandmother, who were never a part of our arguments with Herm's parents about the marriage, flew down to Philadelphia for the engagement party. After a two-month separation, I was genuinely glad to see them. They met a number of the Hubers' friends, all of whom had similar stories of immigration and desperate survival. They were all new immigrants. As I made my way around the living and dining room, observing, mingling, I was really happy to see my father smiling and my mother having a good time feasting on the good food Pesche and I had prepared.

The engagement party was also an opportunity to meet some of Herm's friends, many of whom I would not see again until their 50th high school reunion. We received many thoughtful gifts such as a large tray made of the newest plastic (wave of the future), à la *The Graduate*, Mexican crystal wine glasses that we still use although they are foggy now, and an ice bucket that played music! We were also given cash gifts, totaling an amazing (at that time) $158 for our new joint account. My parents also gave Herm an elegant gold Longines watch as an engagement gift. His parents gave me a diamond watch. They were both beautiful and thoughtful gifts, which may have been coordinated by them without our knowledge or were simply the parental engagement gift de rigueur. At the time, we were afraid to actually wear the watches: they were the most valuable things we owned. Today, Herm no longer has his watch. He gave it to our first son-in-law, Mike, as a wedding gift. Mine has long since stopped working. Fortunately, the marriage far outlasted the gifts.

At the engagement party in Philadelphia with Sandu, Netty, Mamaia, and the happy couple, summer 1968.

In a letter a few months after I returned to Montreal in the fall, Herm wrote, "Believe me Moishe wants us to get married, and he loves you with all his heart." Moishe was so overcome with the fact of our engagement and Herm's leaving the home for graduate school, he was simply unprepared for it to hit all at once. Herm said that his father was "mad at himself for becoming so blindly attached to us."

Herm was reassuring himself that we could remain close to his parents after marriage if we corresponded with them regularly, called, and visited once in a while. He seemed also to want confirmation that my parents were facing the same agonies of their child leaving home. "My parents have a happy relationship and they'll feel lonely; I just hate to imagine how your parents will feel," he wrote.

Without intending to, he tapped into my concerns, some voiced and some not, about leaving my family in Canada. I thought he was also expressing some of his own doubts and guilt about taking me away from them. Mostly though, I was really looking forward to running away from a life that had become increasingly difficult. The future could only be better.

It was no secret that there was much tension in my home. My father went through a devastating bankruptcy while I was in high school. We lived only on my mother's salary from Woolworth's, which made Sandu feel worse and worse about himself. He drank more as their relationship deteriorated and he became more embittered and remote. My parents helplessly looked to me to find solutions for their problems. For example, I had to sit in on their meetings with their accountant to help make decisions. I had neither the skills nor experience to make them, and it burdened me with impossible responsibility; I felt overwhelmed and trapped. Thus, whenever they tried to parent me thereafter, I rebelled. I screamed and yelled, which only escalated as I got older. In fact, it might even be accurate to say that I terrorized them. I think they were eager to see me marry and leave, expecting some peace and quiet. I couldn't wait to do so, though not without some guilt about abandoning them.

Also, I was increasingly responsible for my grandmother. Her vision had worsened even as I continued to watch her inject herself daily with insulin. It was my job to check that there was always a Coca Cola under the kitchen sink for her to drink when her sugar dropped too low. I also took care of her in other ways. When she could no longer see the dials on the stove and oven, it was my job to check they were turned off. I also cooked her meals and regularly washed and set her hair, which I enjoyed. I realized that Mamaia would be the only one who would unconditionally miss me, as I would miss her.

Chapter Nineteen

A WEDDING

I RETURNED to my second year at McGill with even less interest than I'd had at the end of my first year, skipping most of my classes, and just barely doing the work. I thought the policy of mandatory attendance was ridiculous, and foolishly ignored it. When I was not playing cards, I was daydreaming about our upcoming wedding. There is no doubt that I was being reckless, but I was obsessed with wedding plans. My parents didn't know what I was doing. Nor did I listen to Herm when he tried to scold me into being more responsible. I was exercising some very bad judgment and doing what I was starting to do best, defying authority.

I still have vivid memories of sitting on top of a card table in the Student Lounge, my left arm extended in front of me, showing off my diamond ring as I imitated Barbra Streisand singing in the movie, *Funny Girl.* "Sadie, Sadie, married lady, see what's on my hand...." I often try to sing it to my grandchildren, but they mercifully lose interest before we get to the juicy parts—"The honeymoon was such delight, that we got married that same night...."

I did go to class occasionally. Once I missed a mid-term because I was totally unprepared. The next day, wearing one of those popular 1960s tent dresses that made everyone look pregnant, I went to see the compassionate, middle-aged female professor. I sheepishly asked for an extension for "personal reasons." I did not lie. Nor did I correct her misconception. She gave me the extension. In the end, none of that helped. I ended up with four D's despite the fact that I read the material and studied for the exams. Another professor, an American draft dodger, had announced at the beginning of the semester that he found mandatory attendance unnecessary. He gave me a "B." When I questioned each of the other professors about the grade, they all had the same response—"It should have been an 'F' due to your lack of attendance, but you did well on the exams, hence the D." I felt very depressed, and a failure, but I knew it was all my own fault. Getting married and leaving Montreal and McGill would be a big relief. As it turned out, I had to do a lot of explaining when I applied to Rutgers University for my next year, and to the law school admissions office ten years later.

While I was pre-occupied with wedding plans, Herm was worried and overwhelmed about graduate school. He was concerned that he would not be admitted into a good school, the only ones that offered programs in experimental psychopathology, his primary area of interest. He even applied to Canadian universities in his field.

There were many who opposed the Vietnam War and the mandatory conscription of men over the age of 18. There were deferments available, such as one for males matriculated in an accredited college as a full time undergraduate student. Many others, unable to obtain a deferment, went through extremes to avoid the draft. We heard of people with allergies to wool, rubbing their feet with mild acid solutions to simulate severe allergic reactions to military socks.

Herm's family was terrified he might be drafted. Herm and I worried, too. Most people we knew were worried. Once he graduated from Temple, Herm would no longer be eligible for a student deferment.

Herm wrote about a touching, yet heart breaking incident relating to his parents' fears about the Vietnam War. His father suddenly came to his room, stood by his desk wordlessly, his face contorted with tears. Herm followed his father into his room and sat next to him on his bed, his arm around his father's shoulders, while his father cried, "Like I've never seen any man cry before. I was talking to him the whole time, trying to soothe him, and he couldn't even answer.... Finally, he calmed down a little and we talked a little...."

"Anyway, my father said that the main reason he was crying was because he is scared to death of the draft... and my going to Vietnam.... But, there's nothing to do at the present time since we have to wait until May or June when I graduate & we'll see how the war, the new president, and the draft are doing then," he wrote.

Not my style at all. When I am facing a problem, I need to deal with it right then and there. Otherwise, I cannot stop ruminating until I find a way to address the issue. Herm is a big-time procrastinator. He did, however, unwittingly find a solution.

At a doctor's visit, Herm was reminded that he suffers from a bone disease that affects his knees, Osgood-Schlatter's Disease, which would disqualify him from serving in the military. It is a disorder involving painful inflammation of the growth plates of the lower front of the knee, where the large tendon attaches to the lower portion of the kneecap and which then attaches to the shinbone. As a teenager, he'd suffered greatly with knee pain, and needed casts on his knees for a time, but had less distress as an adult. A doctor's note and a copy of the x-rays was all the Draft Board required. All that worrying for nothing.

My grandmother's greatest concern was that she be able to walk down the aisle with us. It loomed large when she was suddenly hospitalized for unstable sugar levels. Herm's response was unexpected: "I really care for your grandmother; she has so much of the level-headedness and ability to bring up children that unfortunately is lacking in your parents. I think you're lucky your grandmother has been usually around to counteract the nervousness and coldness generated by your mother and father, respectively." I was really surprised that Herm had picked up on this because my parents were usually on their best behavior when he was present. He was right, of course, which I didn't fully realize until after I got to see how his family interacted.

Our wedding was to be in Montreal, paid for by the small reparation that was paid to my mother by the German government when I was about twelve. She had invested the money for my future wedding. Now that the time approached, even calm and unflappable Herm began to get excited, "Well, here I am and there you are; but soon, Kaboom. It's really hard to believe that soon us two punks will be married 'together with 'presha'." (Herm's father fondly observed us when we lived in their home before the wedding. He commented, "One goes upstairs, the other one goes upstairs. One comes downstairs, the other one comes downstairs. They're always together with pressure.")

Shopping for a wedding dress wholesale at one of the Montreal factories recommended by my mother's friend was painful. The place was dark and crowded, crammed with dresses, with only one elderly saleswoman to help, and of course, none of my friends. What should have been fun turned into a dismal experience.

I settled on a gown I never really liked, but my mother insisted it would do the job. Although she did not love it either, it was all we could afford. The gown had a lacey bodice, sleeveless with no collar, ending in a simple waist that met a full skirt, not a princess full, just full. Neither flattering to my figure nor to my neck, it turned me into a giraffe! We bought it just a few weeks before I went to Lenny's wedding where his petite, beautiful bride, Sarita, wore a lovely gown. I couldn't have worn the kind of gown she wore, but there were plenty of flattering styles beyond my reach.

In addition to wedding preparations, there were marriage preparations, a trousseau. My mother and I shopped for bedding and linens, but my mother decided we would make our own feather pillows from two huge feather pillows we'd brought from Israel, each about 48-inches square. We figured out one of those would yield two normal-size pillows. As we went about it, we recreated a mess as funny as the wine-making scene in *I Love Lucy* where Lucy is stomping grapes in a low wine barrel. Hilarious!

To make the pillows, we locked ourselves in the bathroom, wearing nothing but underwear. As we emptied all the feathers from the large pillow, we tried unsuccessfully to contain all of them in the old bathtub. Then came the problem of filling each of the new pillowcases as feathers flew wildly all around the bathroom. As we chased them around laughing hysterically, feathers infiltrated our hair, noses and eyes. We were both covered in feathers by the time we finished, looking like disheveled chickens. It took days to get rid of the excess feathers, but I still have the pillows we made, re-covered a few times over the years. Some of our guests even ask for them.

My mother was frugal, always afraid to spend what little there was, but in a surprising gesture she took me to her favorite department store, Eaton's, to buy a negligee set for my honeymoon. It was the most beautiful thing I had ever worn. All in beige silk with little adornment, it was a long nightgown with a robe to match. My mother was much more interested in this purchase than in the wedding gown. Needless to say, I never wore it for more than a few minutes at a time.

I received Herm's last letter, posted on April 29, 1969, already celebrating the end of a phase and the beginning of a new one. "Well, I think this may be the last letter I'll ever write to you (I hope)."

The ceremony and reception both took place at our synagogue on Cote-des-Neiges. Coincidently, our rabbi was the brother of one of Herm's high school teachers. It was a pink and red affair with a large turnout including my Aunt Lontzi who traveled all night by bus from

New York City. She had flown in from San Paulo at the last minute, delayed by a hard-to-get visa. She did the same thing four years later to see my first baby, spending less than twelve hours with us. In addition, Pesche's only surviving nephew, Shimon had traveled with his wife all the way from Argentina. And Moishe's nephew Shmilke, who had immigrated to Palestine before the war, came from New York City.

My cousin Anna, a bridesmaid at my wedding.

Herm's brother, Lenny, was best man and his new bride, Sarita, was my matron of honor. My maid of honor was my cousin, Anna. Yes, the same cousin who ignored me on the school playground. My mother, in a borrowed pink gown and my father in a rented suit, smiled little as they walked down the aisle, and looked very somber during the entire affair. I don't think they could believe they were actually there without worrying about some last-minute problem.

The traditional Jewish wedding ceremony began with our signing of the ketubah (marriage contract), witnessed by Sandu and Lenny, in a private space. I then walked down the aisle toward the chupah (wedding canopy) to the music of one of my favorite Hebrew songs, *Erev Shel Shoshanim* (Evening of Roses) played by my former piano teacher, Mr. Andre.

Herm was waiting before the chupah where he met me and raised my veil, folding it back during the unveiling (to make sure he was marrying the right bride), another Jewish custom. God forbid I was the wrong one! Not that there was another one available. I circled the groom seven times. The vows themselves were very moving and Herm had tears in his eyes, probably out of relief—his letter-writing days were finally over. Next, Herm broke the glass. "Mazel tov," shouted the guests.

A reception followed in the synagogue's party room, a simple space with a white painted wooden fence along the back wall. We sat just in front of it at a rectangular head table with our parents and other immediate relatives. In front of us, on the dessert table, was a large bouquet of pink and red carnations, and white daffodils. Our friends and relatives sat at tables in front of that.

During the reception, I was endlessly called upon by staff to answer questions. I wish someone had imparted to me the wisdom I shared with our daughters for their weddings about thirty years later: "Only you know what everything is supposed look like and how it is meant to work out. None of the guests do. So, they will not be disappointed. You have hired competent, experienced staff. Leave it all to them and enjoy yourself."

Ann and Herm walking back up the aisle after the ceremony.

As Herm and I mingled among the guests, the most frequently asked question was, "Where are you going for your honeymoon?" "Quebec City for a week," we answered with nervous excitement. "We are going to spend our first night at the Chateau Champlain in Montreal and tomorrow we will take a bus to Quebec City."

We originally planned an exciting and adventurous honeymoon, and had spent months researching a motorcycle trip through Europe, following the philosophy expressed in a popular travel guide—*Europe on $10 a Day*. We thought we could write a book about our travels in Europe on a motorcycle.

When we started to explore the airfare, however, Lenny began to question our judgment. At first, we decided to ignore his advice which we felt was wrong for us and went ahead and bought tickets, borrowing the money from Herm's parents. Lenny, however, does not give up that easily either, having been sewn from the same cloth as his brother. He continued to nag us. In his view, it was frivolous to go off to Europe for a few weeks when we had no place to live in New Jersey, where Herm would be attending graduate school at Rutgers, no job and little money to count on besides Herm's assistantship. In our view, we could take care of these things when we returned. Since we were starting with nothing, what difference did it make if we started with nothing a few weeks later?

Eventually and grudgingly, we came to the conclusion that he was probably right and surrendered our tickets. We could not get a refund. To our surprise and great relief, Herm's parents graciously never said a word about the money they had loaned us for the tickets.

In retrospect, I think perhaps we should have followed our own instincts. For many years, I deeply regretted that we did not go on a trip that would have been so meaningful for us. We have since traveled to many places where we had wonderful and interesting times; Morocco, Italy, Spain, England, Ireland, and more recently Poland, Germany, and Romania, but our dream adventure at the beginning of our married life could never be recaptured.

When it was time for us to leave the wedding, I changed into a green suit with a short skirt and a matching wide-brimmed hat. I loved that outfit, much more than my wedding gown. As we said our goodbyes and hugged so many friends and relatives, Mamaia started to cry. Soon, everyone else was crying, including Mr. Andre, my music teacher. A photograph of me hugging my grandmother is memorable for my aunt Lily standing next to us, holding back tears. Behind me is

Ann kissing Mamaia goodbye after the wedding.

one of my parents' friends smiling. He was the person who taught me to dance when I was twelve. I was not just getting married, but I was leaving the country.

Sandu and Netty only came to visit us in New Jersey once, in the fall of 1969 for a short visit after a long and dusty overnight bus ride. Sadly, Sandu was diagnosed with liver cancer a year later, prompting us to make a trip to Montreal. When we saw him, I was surprised that he showed no visible signs of ill health and it was hard for me to believe that we would lose him so quickly. My mother had called to tell us he was in a great pain, but he still had his ruddy complexion and had not lost weight. I hadn't lost anyone but my grandfather Carol, who died when I was so young; I didn't know what to expect. Intellectually, I knew it would be a huge loss but I didn't anticipate the emptiness I would feel.

I had always believed that Sandu loved me. When I was small, he'd held my hand on our weekly Saturday outings to the park. As I approached puberty, he became more uncomfortable in my presence and grew more distant. He would blush if he had to speak to me directly about my skirt being too short. But the smile he had for me was his broadest, and his touch gentle. He was not a hugger or a kisser, but no one in my family was demonstratively affectionate. There was obvious love in the way he crowed proudly about me to others—I was the brightest, the best, the smartest. That pedestal was so high, he thought McGill would have no choice but to accept me into their mighty university.

Everything happened so fast—only about eight weeks from symptoms to the end. There was so little time to adjust. Fortunately, I was able to visit him one more time. I stayed with him at the hospital for a couple of days towards the very end of his illness. He lay in a private room, supported high on pillows, with intravenous tubes running across the bed. If I tried to sit on the bed to hold his warm hands, he would wince in pain. Even in pain, he smiled at me as I sat on a chair in the corner of the room, watching me as I studied for a test from a heavy textbook, probably biology. He extracted a deathbed promise from me to graduate from college, a promise I kept, and even did one better—graduating from law school after I had given birth to three children. I promised him, repeatedly, I would do so. He made no other demands on me just as he never had in life. When I left, I kissed him on his deeply furrowed forehead as tears rolled down both our cheeks. That's my last memory of him.

Herm and I drove to Montreal for the funeral only a week or so later. It was a small one, attended by a few family friends and his sister Lily's family. Mamaia, Lily, and I seemed to be doing most of the crying. As I stood in the cold, staring at the freshly dug earth and a new layer of snow, I did not know why I was crying or what I was feeling. My mother was stone-faced. I thought she was in shock. We sat shiva (mourning period) in Montreal for the first day but then had to leave, after the third eight-inch snowstorm of the season.

A profound sadness hit me after I returned home, for all that he missed out on with such an early death, like seeing me graduate from college, then law school, and meeting his grandchildren. He would have loved the freedom of grandchildren in a way he could not enjoy the love of a child because of the responsibility.

Not long after Sandu's death, we went to see the movie *La Strada* that left me helplessly sobbing at its end. My father, as he aged, started to look a lot like Anthony Quinn in that role. And like Quinn's character who was ambitious but deeply flawed, failed, and closed off, Sandu's life was filled with sadness and unfulfilled dreams, which I felt profoundly after he was gone.

I don't know what Sandu wanted or expected out of life. I don't know what any of them wanted. They struggled for so many years just to survive—to achieve safety. Then the struggle turned to providing a roof over their heads with the other necessities like food and clothing for all of us. I can't imagine what else they aspired to other than financial security. We never had a house, or a car, or took vacations other than the two my mother and I took to Atlantic City. My parents' life after the war was never as affluent as it had been before. Financial security never came to my father. There were no savings at his death, but a small insurance policy that paid for the funeral, a fur coat for my mother, and a small loan to Herm and me for our first house. Netty did not want us to repay the loan. I still have her fur coat.

Ten months after Sandu died my mother remarried without even telling us because she was embarrassed at how little time had passed.

She met Simon at a synagogue meeting of "Parents Without Partners." She was still young, 48, and fell in love, I think. He was an electrician and more financially stable than Sandu, though he was a gambler. Simon also was a survivor, a concentration camp escapee, who had only been previously married in the "camps," went to Israel, and followed a wealthy friend to Montreal, who'd promised to give him work. Netty's quality of life improved a bit as a result of that marriage. They lived in her apartment, Simon had a car and they would come down to see us a few times a year. Simon liked my family and me and turned out to be a caring grandfather.

My mother's life only saw more financial stability after Herm and I achieved some financial stability ourselves, when we were able to help provide for her, about 20 years into our marriage, just in time for our daughters' college educations and weddings.

Chapter Twenty

ISRAEL, AT LAST

AFTER OUR GLORIOUS honeymoon in Quebec City, where housekeeping had to wait each morning for us to leave the marital bed, and where Herm ate his first non-kosher food (spare ribs), we returned to Montreal to my parents' apartment. But we were unable to leave for the United States as planned. I had applied for an immigrant visa based on my marriage to an American citizen. However, it had not yet come through, reportedly because the Romanian quota was filled. About a week later, we were allowed to fly to Philadelphia.

My previous retail experience in Montreal's Woolworth's store became a ticket to a job in the Woolworth's store at the Bala Cynwyd Shopping Center, where I started a job as a cashier. I brought a letter of recommendation to the manager and started work the next day. Two months later, I guiltily quit. My new role was to support Herm's graduate studies in psychology at Rutgers University as I continued my studies at night, but now in New Brunswick, New Jersey.

We moved to a first floor apartment in a two-family house, near the Rutgers campus. Unrealistic to our core, we thought we might develop the same relationship with our landlord that Herm's family had with Florence and Charlie, but nothing could have been further from the truth. Our landlords were over-controlling meddlers who regularly entered our apartment to see what we were up to whenever our shoes or boots were not outside our door. We tricked them once by taking our footwear into the apartment and waiting for them to come in. You can imagine their surprise; however, they were neither embarrassed nor apologetic. They just retreated.

With $600 in wedding gifts and a little earnings from our summer jobs, we paid our security deposit (the first month's rent of $100) and bought some furniture: a bed with a headboard that matched the cheap double dresser trimmed with plastic faux wood, a used black and white television, a used small couch with matching chair both covered in Naugahyde (black fake leather), a white outdoor wrought iron table and two chairs with blue plastic seat cushions, and a $10 homemade cabinet we found at a house sale, which we painted blue and white. The cabinet always had sentimental value because the widow from whom we bought it explained that her husband had made it early in their 60-year marriage. Moving day was August 1 with a U-Haul and our trusty haulers, Moishe, Pesche, and their neighbors Florence, and Charlie.

I landed a job as a service representative at New Jersey Bell Telephone Company. I had initially applied to be a telephone operator but thankfully was rejected. "You're too smart to be just an operator," someone said after a full day of testing. Everything seemed to be working out as planned.

The yearning to see Israel again never went away. After our marriage, I often spoke about my need to go back. Finally, Herm's response was a challenge—"If you really feel the need to go, you can do something about it." So, I did.

I was the main wage earner since Herm only had a small research assistantship. It was up to me. One day at lunchtime, I walked around the corner from the New Jersey Bell office where I worked and opened up a vacation club account at the nearest bank. Fifty dollars out of every paycheck went to the account until we had enough money for the airfare. I knew we would not need any hotel money. We had lots of relatives who would and did put us up. It was 1973 and we were expecting our first child.

It was exhilarating to be back in Israel. Everything felt so comfortable and natural, including my pregnant ride in the side bucket of a motorcycle owned of one of Herm's cousins, also named Moishe Huber, who drove us around Tel Aviv in his only mode of transportation. We slept in his teenage children's beds while they were off on their mandatory military service.

My mother's cousin Shelley also put us up on folding beds on her balcony in Haifa. Her apartment was so small that there was barely enough room for two stools to accommodate us for the Seder table at the holiday. But being there for Passover was so special because we visited so many of the places we'd read about like the Dead Sea and Masada.

In Haifa, I found a small, black and white picture, depicting a young child dressed in an Israeli kibbutz uniform: blue short shorts, button down short-sleeved shirt, white short socks inside scuffed laced, leather shoes and the obligatory bell-shaped sunhat. It brought back such fond memories of my own childhood. I had worn the same outfit and imagined that if I were having a child in Israel, she would wear it, too.

Even now, whenever I do go back to Israel to visit, just landing at Tel Aviv airport brings back great joy despite the fact that so many years have passed and the country has changed so much. I always get a kick out of responding to Israeli security officers, in Hebrew, "I don't speak Hebrew. I forgot how." They always compliment my native accent, and it makes me feel proud.

After giving birth to Rebecca, the tiny light of our lives, I left New Jersey Bell and took a job as a legal secretary for a young lawyer opening his first office. Herm and I met him during the closing on our first home. I'd asked him very brazenly, "You wouldn't happen to have a part-time job, would you?"

"Can you type?" he asked.

"So-so," I motioned with my hand. I hadn't learned to type in high school because I was finally transferred out of the dummy class. Herm had taught me so I could help with his doctoral dissertation.

"What about shorthand? Can you take shorthand?"

"Well," I said, "I don't know shorthand but I did learn speed writing at New Jersey Bell."

Imagine my surprise when he said, "You look like you have a good head on your shoulders. You're hired."

As I set up the young attorney's office and began learning the work, my typing improved and soon I became his right hand. I also began to think again about the possibility of becoming a lawyer—the dream I abandoned at age 14 when Sandu told me that girls don't get admitted to law school.

As a legal secretary, I met many other young male members of the bar whose competence I found questionable. I often came home, exasperated. "If that schmuck can do it, why can't I?" I thought to myself. Eventually, I verbalized that thought.

On a quiet New Year's Eve a year or so later, at home with rare time on our hands, Herm and I came to the decision that I should indeed go to law school even though we now had a second wonderful child, Rayna. We both realized that I was happier working than staying at home. Now it was Herm's turn to put *me* through school. We wanted some flexibility in our careers. Our goal was to be professionals and eventually to retire together.

On a cold and rainy in February, I went back to Rutgers in New Brunswick to take the LSATs, needed for admission to law school. It felt strange and awkward to be back on campus. As I looked around the classroom I realized that, at age 27, I was substantially older than the other test-takers. I felt that old familiar pang of not belonging, but I was determined to give it a try. There was no time to waste. I was thrilled to be admitted to both Rutgers Law School—Newark (a public university) and Seton Hall Law School (a private school) after my pitiful college record at McGill, although my later transcripts and LSAT scores were pretty good. Once I was accepted, I started to make preparations to go. As fate would have it, I had to postpone my attendance for another two years to give birth to our third child, Sara, the unexpected blessing.

As a result of the delay, I forfeited my original admissions. Two years later, I had to retake the LSATs to reapply. This time, I was again accepted at Seton Hall, the pricey private school, but only wait-listed at Rutgers Law School—Newark. By the first day of school, we still hadn't figured out how we were going to pay for it. When I returned home, Herm was desperately waiting for me, telephone in hand.

"Quick, quick, you have to call Rutgers Admissions before 4:00 p.m. They are accepting you off the waiting list but you have to call before they call the next person." I called immediately. It was going to be Rutgers Law School after all!

We then took some very daring steps. Although we had a mortgage and three children now, we both quit our jobs so I could go to school while Herm looked after the children during the day. I managed to get a student loan even though they had become scarce during the Reagan administration; I was off and running in a beat-up old Volkswagen bug with neither air conditioning nor heat. We were not totally reckless because Herm had already started a private practice in the evening by then and was seeing a couple of patients every day when I returned home from class.

I loved law school. I thrived on the intellectual stimulation, the adrenaline rush of legal argument, and the camaraderie of a study group of wonderful women, all of whom were a little older than I and supportive. By then, I was a 30-year-old woman, which only made me more determined, organized, and efficient. Truthfully, it was easier to go to law school with three children than it ever was to work with three children. My schedule was more predictable and I had more control over it. Those were probably the three best years of my life.

Even though I did well and excelled among my study group, my insecurities rose up again after I failed to make the cut for the Law Review. I was disappointed, too, in the responses I received for my summer internships, although I did land a good local one. By then it was time to apply for a job. Unsure of myself, I shied away from the bigger, better-known firms, and went after the less prestigious positions. At one interview, I was horrified when the interviewer spent the entire time looking up and down my legs.

Eventually, I landed an associate's job in a small firm with a high reputation—I'll call them Baum, Cohen, and Schwartz—an *Irish* firm in a shopping center near home. The location turned out to be perfect, next to a theater and a Burger King. Periodically, I'd leave my children at a movie while I worked. They could just walk next door to my office when they were done watching and eating.

On my first day at the law firm, I arrived in a new suit, and in a display of pulling rank, was stiffly greeted at the door by one of the partners, my future colleague. "Hello, Ann," he said. "I'm Mr. Schwartz."

My sharp-tongued response to this power play was swift—"Hello, Mr. Schwartz, I'm *Mrs.* Huber." He was unaccustomed to working with a female lawyer, and was never comfortable even talking to me. I wonder what he thought of the 3' x 4' framed photograph I hung in my office. It was an original, taken in the 1940s, of Radcliffe women students, all dressed in pretty white dresses with corsages, pulling an old wooden wagon on what must have been their graduation day. The late 19th century wagon was covered with fading slogans such as, "8,000,000 Working Women need the Vote for Equal pay for Equal Work and All Labor Legislation," and "90% of Teachers Are Women. Our Nation Needs Intelligent Voters." Some things hadn't changed much in a hundred years.

My mentor at the firm was a great and seasoned trial lawyer who taught me the difference between getting it done and producing good quality legal work. He also warned me that if I tried to please all the partners, it would burn me out. I didn't heed his warning. I started to work too hard, spending too many hours trying to please too many people, slowly exhausting myself. At the same time, I was striving to be a supermom to my children. I went back to work every evening, after making dinner and helping with homework. I left work for a time most afternoons to drive one or more of the children to dance class, music class, track practice, whatever. Herm worked evenings seeing patients. A neighborhood teen babysat for the girls.

After my fourth year at the firm, working on cases I really enjoyed, I returned from a three-week vacation to find that I could no longer continue at that pace. I decided to leave the firm to spend some time with my children. Following a short break and another short-term position, I again took the safe route, and opened my own practice. That was not and is not the way to get ahead. Most of the firms in New Jersey are solo practices and all of them struggle to attract good clients.

It occurred to me that running for public office would give me some free advertising and help me meet important people. Boy, was I surprised to learn that I actually like politics! Unfortunately, I also found that spending time campaigning added another stressor to my life, and I also had to struggle to overcome unchanging facts: I was a Democratic female candidate running for public office in a Republican stronghold.

I was defeated in three straight election cycles. But I found my voice and I persisted and was elected a Councilwoman in Randolph. A few years later, I was appointed to be Mayor by the Council. Four years later I was re-elected. That child from the dummy class was moving on up!

It was a thrilling time. I loved the political dialogue, the maneuvering in building coalitions to get legislation passed. I was fascinated by the issues and savored learning more and more about each. Having a political debate was just as exhilarating for me as arguing a case or an appeal. My tolerant daughters, while never appreciating having a spotlight on the family, always played their roles, smiling and being polite. They came every time I asked them to participate in a function and held the Bible for me when I was sworn into office. I don't know if they ever asked any of their friends to tell their parents to vote for me, but I do know they were proud of me.

Even winning election and re-election did not provide all the self-confidence I still lacked. But, my private law practice took me a step further. I made a good enough living so that Herm and I could educate our daughters and see them off into successful careers and marriages. I then sold my practice and joined the New Jersey Attorney General's Office. It was there that I finally reached my potential, after our daughters were grown and married, when I had the time and freedom to do my best legal work. It took some time but eventually, my colleagues and superiors began to recognize and reward me for my accomplishments. I was buoyed by their praises. Herm was always there whenever I needed a boost, and was the first to recognize that I had finally found the place with the right combination of conditions to make me feel better about myself.

Only fifty years after I arrived in Montreal, after a life driven by an unrelenting need to prove myself to myself, did I find some relief, satisfaction, and most importantly, peace.

Chapter Twenty-One

KEEPING SECRETS

WHEN WE WERE in our mid fifties, Herm and I felt we wanted
to know more about our parents' experiences during the War. So
we decided to videotape each of our mothers telling her story. Still
beautiful at age eighty, my mother sat calmly on her living room
couch, while Herm set up the camera. I admired the way her short
white curly hair framed the soft skin of her wrinkled face. "So, tell
us where you were living when the war started," Herm asked. To my
shock, she asked him to turn off the video recorder and leave the
apartment, an embarrassed, shy smile on her face. Turning to me, she
said, as she had mysteriously many times in those last few years, "There
is something I need to tell you before I die." I was ready. Or I thought
I was.

"The Romanian army wasn't any good and Germany took over,"
she began. "Sandu was allowed to return to re-join the family. We, your
grandparents and Lontzi, like Jews living in other Romanian cities,
were forced to report to labor camps every day." She sighed and took a
big breath before continuing. "We were demeaned and made to wear
the yellow star on the outside of our clothing. Food was rationed," my
mother remembered.

The exact date of my father's return is a mystery, but on the 1942 census of men, my grandfather is the only male listed in the household. There is no record of my father. By 1944, Antonescu's government was overthrown by King Michael and the Russians. The Romanians then fought alongside the Russians to defeat Germany.

"Slowly, painfully, the war years passed and eventually, life returned to normal under the Russian occupation, as normally as one could live under a brutal dictatorship," my mother explained.

She shifted in her seat, "Shortly after the war ended, the family decided that Sandu and I would move to Bucharest to open our own shoe store to take advantage of the post war, booming economy." My mother always referred to my father by his given name rather than as "your father." My grandfather still had a stock of leather shoes and boots, with a readily available supply from contacts developed over many years. Leather was the commodity of choice and leather goods were much sought after by the occupying Russian soldiers. "We assumed, correctly, that the demand would be even greater in Bucharest."

My grandparents and my parents with me in our home in Bucharest only a few months before we left Romania.

Mamaia sold her house in Galati so that my parents could buy a house in Bucharest. Proof of home ownership was a requirement for moving into the city, but soon after my parents bought the house, all privately owned housing was confiscated by the Communist regime; residents and businesses were allowed to remain in place. The business flourished. Pictures of the family in 1950 show a well-dressed family of parents, and grandparents, doting on their infant granddaughter, me.

"To maintain the store's leather stock, Sandu and I took turns traveling back and forth by train between Bucharest and Galati," my mother went on. "On one such trip, I was approached by the owner of the shop across the street from my grandfather's shoe store. Marcel was much older than me, but still a handsome, friendly and vivacious man." Like Sandu, he was dark skinned, had dark eyes and even a widow's peak. Unlike Sandu, Marcel seemed sophisticated. My mother described herself as "a shy twenty-four-year old, very pretty but also very naïve." Where was this story leading?

"By the time I turned sixteen, I had known Sandu for more than seven years," she continued. "When I was about 15 years old, he took advantage of me. I thought no other man would want me and had no choice but to marry him. I was so naïve. But I can tell you that I never loved him." I was shocked. Over the years I had come to realize that she no longer loved him but—never loved him? That was hard to believe.

As a child, I didn't understand that many of my mother's behaviors did not necessarily emanate from love. She'd always been terrified of upsetting my father and catered to his every whim, such as being home by a certain time, making his favorite food or keeping non-kosher salami hidden in a corner of the refrigerator for him. On the other hand, it seemed to me that my father worshiped the ground on which she walked. He was very jealous every time my mother spoke to another man, even the manager at the store where she worked. Numerous times, I remember my father bringing home very expensive gifts such as a new vacuum cleaner, crystal vase, fur hat—none of which we could afford. I realized now that they were bribes for her affection. These thoughts raced through my brain as I squirmed in my seat during this very uncomfortable conversation.

"But," she continued, "that's why I was so willing to respond to Marcel's advances." She smiled as she recounted how Marcel promised to show her a good time, such as she had never before enjoyed. They frequented restaurants, went to the movies, to concerts and to Yiddish theater. This was culture she had never known. It did not take long before a love affair flourished, despite the fact that they were both married.

"Marcel had two children, almost grown. We were happily together for over three years." They took turns traveling to wherever my father was not. But, their love affair crashed in the summer of 1949 when my mother discovered that she was pregnant with Marcel's child.

"How did you know it was his child?" I asked.

"Sandu didn't want any children and took precautions to prevent it. I was scared, at first. I was already an aunt to Lontzi's son, Mircea, whom I loved and I wanted my own child—something Sandu did not want. I didn't want an abortion." Orphaned by his mother's death, my father always wanted to be the center of attention. At least that's what my mother had always told me. His insecurity was palpable, threatened by the idea that my mother might love another, even a child.

When my mother realized she was pregnant, she confided in my grandparents that she was planning to leave my father. (I still refer to him as my father, even after learning about Marcel.) This must have been a double shock for her parents, Mamaia and Tataia, having known and loved Sandu. My grandparents counseled against leaving, unlike parents in other cultures who might have ostracized her. "How would you manage as an unmarried woman with a child? How could you support yourself? Who would want a woman with a child?" They advised her to take this secret to her grave. And she almost did.

My mother bravely made the most important choice she would ever make to live with it. Little pain or sadness showed now on her face as she told me that Sandu never knew that I was not his daughter. She let him believe it was a failure of birth control.

"How did you do that?" I asked.

"We had been away on a trip and had marital relations. Later, I told him that his precautions must not have worked."

How ironic that a man as jealous as Sandu apparently never questioned her explanation! As emotionally devastating and practically complicated as these events must have been for her, my mother never told Marcel either. I always thought I looked like Sandu. My oldest daughter has Sandu's dark skin, his same dark eyes and curly hair, even his widow's peak. I was determined to learn whether or not this story was true. Surely, it was not true and nothing more than another sign of dementia. Even if she'd had an affair, I could still be Sandu's child. I wanted to be his child.

"I never spoke to him again," my mother told me. "Nor did I ever see him again. Though I did get tidbits of information about him from my cousin Shelley." She would see him periodically in Haifa where he too, immigrated with his family. I wonder whether he ever got bits of information about me from Shelley and ever wondered why he never heard from Netty again. She kept her painful secret for the next fifty-five years, and after the death of my grandparents, not a single other person in the world knew the truth until now.

When my mother told me all this, I was stunned. I had two fathers, neither of whom would ever truly know me. My head was spinning. I couldn't decide whether to laugh or to cry. I did both. I was shaking with anger when I left her apartment. How could she have kept this from me? Part of me wished she had never told me. It shook my very foundation.

As soon as I settled down a little bit, I decided on a course of action. I called my paternal cousin, Anna. As I told her this crazy story, I was surprised that she took it in stride, without judgment. Her first words were, "So, Netty had an affair, eh?" as she chuckled.

"Please don't say anything to Lily," I said. "She will always be my aunt regardless."

"No problem." I asked Anna to take a DNA test with me. "Just tell me what I need to do," she responded. "I can't believe it. You look like Sandu."

"I can't believe it either," I told her.

Two weeks later the results arrived. As I held the report in my shaking hands, heart pounding, I couldn't understand the words. My mind had become paralyzed. Herm took the document and said gently, "Sandu is not your biological father." I felt so sad and had to re-assess all my experiences and feelings about Sandu.

My father and I in the park in Haifa. I'm three years old.

As a child, Sandu was always there for me, like a warm comfortable blanket. I have fond memories of him when I was very young, probably about three. They are captured in a photograph of a moment in the park in Haifa. Sandu is crouching down so he can look me straight in the eyes, adoringly, while he holds on to each of my arms with both his warm, soft hands. I have a little smile in return.

I have memories of me, my parents, and grandparents together every Friday night in Israel and then just my parents and I going to the movies on Saturday night. Finding himself in a role he never expected to take on, Sandu and I enjoyed each other's company. I remember just Sandu and I hanging around together in Montreal. In the first few years, when my mother worked on Saturdays and he did not, we spent time walking and talking.

In retrospect, we should have had a very intense bond, but many things started to make sense—like why my relationship with my mother was so much more intense than with my father. I know he loved and cherished me, but she always interfered with our relationship. I did not understand it then, but it was for her own needs that she ran interference, to protect her secrets. I always believed it was because my father had not wanted children, so she and Mamaia always took responsibility for me. Mothers generally do that anyway.

She shielded me from so much. I never really understood why that was necessary except that my father did seem to get angry a lot, frighteningly angry, though he was never violent with any of us.

A few days later, I called Anna. We agreed that we'd grown up as cousins, felt like cousins, and would always be cousins. But I was determined to look for my biological father, even though I had decided Sandu would always be my father. It was not just a father I was searching for, but siblings, something for which I had always longed.

Once again, I went to my mother's apartment on a Saturday afternoon when she was usually willing to chat. This time she told me that Marcel was about twenty years older, and had two children, a girl and boy. It was from her cousin Shelley, with whom she remained close, that my mother learned that Marcel had left Romania for Israel shortly after we emigrated. His son, whose name she did not know, was seventeen years my senior and serving in the Israeli military. "He was a commander," she boasted. She knew nothing about Marcel's daughter who would be about three years younger than her brother. She thought they were living in Tel Aviv.

I asked her, "Do you know if Marcel is still alive?"

"I don't know. After we left Israel, I couldn't keep asking Shelley about Marcel without raising suspicions."

Exasperated, I asked, "Why didn't you tell me sooner? This is so important to me." Perhaps perplexed herself, she would only shrug.

So many times throughout my adult life, she'd alluded to a secret. But she retreated whenever I tried to pry out more information. Now, I ached to know why she hadn't told me sooner. Couldn't she understand that I would want to meet my father, for God's sake? Did she not remember how lonely I felt as a child, and how often I had pleaded for a brother or sister? Apparently, she'd never contemplated the wound her story would inflict on me. Pictures or stories could not bring Marcel to life for me, leaving me filled with deep regret. I needed to know who he was, what he was like. Would he have loved me if he had known me? What genetic influence had he had on me? Knowing the effect an entire childhood filled with my mother's anxieties must have had on me, I was furious. I knew I was loved, but neither my mother nor Sandu were physically affectionate.

Armed with the few details my mother provided, I sought help from Leo, a friend as well as an expert and researcher on the Middle East. Very quickly, he wrote back to tell me that he had found three potential links but couldn't go further without divulging some of my very private information. He wanted to keep me safe. My friend gave me the email addresses for a Londoner whose daughter-in-law was related to me in some way, a woman in Atlanta who he thought was probably a cousin, and a man named David in Israel.

I drafted an email:

Hello,

My name is Ann Avram Huber and I am the friend of L.W. who contacted you on my behalf, inquiring about family connections.

I was recently shocked to find out from my 81-year-old mother that I was born as a result of an extramarital relationship she had with Marcel. My mother, Netty Avram, Nee Marcus, was from Galatz, Romania, as was he.

I was born in Bucharest in 1950. The only thing I know about my biological father is that he would have been born around 1914....

For me, as I'm sure it is for you, family is very important and I am only looking to locate my step siblings and father, if he is still alive, in order to find out as much as possible about a family previously unknown to me. I certainly do not wish to embarrass anyone or cause anyone difficulty, but the possibility of finding family members would be very fulfilling for me, and perhaps to others.

I am asking for your help in making such contacts. If I could enlist your help, I would be quite grateful. Thank you.

Ann

I obsessed for days over different versions and then, I finally sent it.

The Londoner wrote back that he was the father-in-law of a family cousin living in Great Britain. The woman in Atlanta emailed, very excitedly, that she was a cousin, too. And I waited for an answer from David. Would I finally find him, and my father and half sister?

Chapter Twenty-Two

O Brother,
Where Art Thou?

Days passed. I checked email every few hours. Nothing. Was this a silly, fruitless endeavor? Was I misguided to think I could in any way ever undo the mistakes of the past?

Then, suddenly, an email from Israel popped up. Tears streamed down my face as I read the email over and over again:

Dear Ann,

I am just as shocked and surprised as you are, since I am the son of Marcel. So I am probably the half brother you are looking for.

I don't know what to say. Nothing in my life including 30 years of service in the military, has prepared me for such news. Indeed, my father Marcel, my mother, my sister and I, moved from Galatz to Israel in 1950. There is nothing I would like more than exchanging details with you, but please give me some time to digest the news.

One thing which puzzles me is how your mother knows details about us from the time after we moved to Israel (like the fact that I served in the army).

I have many questions and I am sure you must have many too. Please tell me everything you know and let me know what would you want to know.

David

I read it to myself. I read it out loud to Herm and then, almost speechless, I read it out loud again. That sentence still rings in my ears—"I am probably the half brother you are looking for."

Under cross-examination (I am a lawyer, after all), I extracted more details from my mother, and David confirmed that I had found the right family. But indeed, I had missed my chance to ever meet Marcel—he had died about twenty years earlier.

I was prepared to go to Israel to meet David, but David came to me! I was delighted that he would do that. On a business trip to New Jersey, not long after our correspondence began, David and his lovely wife came to our home. He insisted that they travel there on their own, and brought a doll dressed in red velvet for our first grandchild.

The moment I saw him I searched his face for any familiar characteristic I might have noticed on my own, but alas, found none. Soft-spoken, retiring and kindly, he was of average height, slim, with a full head of curly gray hair. He certainly did not look like someone who had defused underwater bombs on the hulls of Israeli ships during his military years.

I found myself strangely scared, awkward, unsure of what to do, to say, how to act. Here was the sibling I always yearned for, hoped for— but what now? I didn't even know how to greet him. Should I kiss him, hug him, shake hands? To be safe, I did all three.

What feelings did I have for him? Could I love him? I'd never even met him. What would we even talk about after we discussed our histories and families? We had no shared experiences, lived continents apart, not to mention the 17-year age difference. I just hoped nature would take me down the right path.

I had prepared dinner for the four of us, but I hadn't invited my mother. She hadn't wanted me to search for him. And, I didn't really want her with us—her negative attitude would drag down the meeting. As we finished our meal, David brought out of his briefcase a photo history and genealogy of the family, which he had compiled for me. It must have taken him many hours to reproduce photographs and carefully annotate them.

We sat side by side as I went through each of the pages and he explained who was in each photograph, filling in some history. Marcel and his wife were first cousins, like my grandparents. They had many of the same cousins. I was emotionally drawn to David by his openness, and felt grateful for his effort, but was disheartened that I found few familiar features in most of the other family members. I did see some resemblance, though, between one of his daughters, Adi, and me in my younger years.

During the course of the evening, I learned that my half-sister died before I knew she existed. But there was still time for him to meet my mother, which he seemed eager to do. The next day, we went to see her. Her only comment was in Romanian which he clearly understood. In her inimitable, unvarnished style enhanced perhaps by her early dementia, she said, "He is not nearly as good-looking as his father."

My mother confirmed that the man in the picture of Marcel fifty years earlier, which David had brought, was indeed Marcel. She and David also shared stories of the street where their fathers' stores had been. Although they were both cordial, I could sense the strain in their conversation. Each reminded the other of disappointment, and although it was unstated, clearly neither wished to see the other again.

I took David's warmth towards me to mean that he was as interested as I was in developing a relationship. Still, we had trouble relating, getting close. We shared nothing but blood. We had nothing in common save my mother. He'd arrived in Israel as an adult. I was only nine months old and of course, had no memories of Romania.

A couple of years later, laden with gifts and David's invitation to stay with him, we traveled to Israel. David and his wife picked us up at the airport and provided us with a private room in their modestly furnished apartment. They lived in one of Tel Aviv's iconic concrete buildings, no more than four stories tall, with small apartments, each with a balcony that also serves as part of the living space. David's sons, the two middle children, came to the apartment to meet us on our first evening. What a delight to meet this previously unknown branch of the family!

We had met Adi, the youngest of the four children, when she'd visited New York six months earlier. We liked each other immediately and a bond began to develop. Adi and her husband were very welcoming in Israel, even took us to the movies one night. It seemed that family ties were strengthening.

We met the extended family at an afternoon barbeque at one of their homes. There, like a Jewish Santa Claus full of enthusiasm, I doled out gifts to all of them, including a hand-crocheted sweater for a new baby. While the family was cordial to us, David's oldest daughter seemed oddly distant. Then the dam broke. She insisted I submit to a DNA test. I was stunned. I held back tears. Did she see me as some kind of scam artist, a thief after David's vast fortune? Insulted, rejected, in my heart I refused the test. But I said, "OK," with a bitter taste in my mouth. Nothing else was said. I expected they would make the arrangements for DNA testing.

We left the next morning. David and I both choked up as we said goodbye. I expected to see him a few months later on his annual business trip to New York.

However, David did not respond to my next email, a thank you for his hospitality. I wrote another email. No response. Perplexed and worried, I waited. Finally, Adi emailed me to explain that my visit had created a painful rift in the family. Perhaps fearful I might be a fraud and up to no good, her sister was still insisting that we take DNA tests. Adi speculated that her sister had been very close to Marcel and could not believe her loving grandfather would have cheated on his wife. I understand this must have been difficult for her. David, stubborn also, was refusing to take the test. Adi told me that until they settled their dispute, David would not communicate with me. Unfortunately, auspicious beginnings sometimes have endings that break the heart.

Sadly, the half-brother who'd once defused bombs, now caught in a family struggle, was not able to defuse this bomb. I haven't heard from David since. It's been nine years. I can only imagine what could have been. Periodically, I do get an email from Adi in which she informs me that David, now in his 80s, is doing well though her mother is suffering from Alzheimer's.

Ultimately, I admire my mother's courage in telling me the terrible truth she kept tightly bound inside her for so many years. I mourn that she waited so long to do so. I also mourn the laughter and joy and pain that siblings might have brought over the years, but it is a life that I could never have had.

Chapter Twenty-Three

FAMILY PILGRIMAGE

SINCE BOTH HERM AND I were born in Europe to families displaced by World War II, much of our history and cultural heritage was lost. Still, we retained a strong sense of what it means to be Jewish. To understand and appreciate what it meant for our parents to be Jewish in their places of birth, and to get more insight into what their lives were like, we had to return to the places of their birth. We did that in a 2010 pilgrimage with our daughter, Rayna, husband Esteban and his parents, Perla and Lito, and grandchild Milo.

Our first stop was to Warsaw, where Pesche had worked in her teens, before it was virtually obliterated by Germany. Its historic center had been recreated brick by brick, following the original architectural plans. It is a beautiful city. There we visited the site of a new Polish Jewish Museum, just a few blocks from the site of Mila 18, the site of an underground bunker where the leaders of the Warsaw Ghetto Uprising committed suicide rather than surrender. The approximate two hundred others escaped from the rear.

In an unexpected and moving event, just as we arrived in the square, an Israeli military unit arrived to sing the Israeli anthem in front of a World War II Memorial. Holding my grandson, singing along, with tears running down my face, I felt that despite the worst Holocaust in history, we had not only survived but could hold our heads high in the land of those who had wished our destruction.

Herm with our grandson Milo in front of the Warsaw World War II Holocaust Memorial, 2010.

From there we headed to Mordy, the shtetl of Moishe and Pesche's stories. We were determined to get there, despite a series of mishaps that included missing the direct train and were compounded by the fact that none of us were able to read the Polish train schedule or announcement board. Surprisingly, none of the ticket clerks understood or spoke English.

Thanks to an English-speaking Scandinavian tourist, we managed to find a train from Warsaw to the transfer stop in the town of Siedlic, the closest point to Mordy. There, randomly and luckily, we happened upon the only English-speaking taxi driver in the town. Fifteen minutes later, the driver pointed out a rusted metal flag on the road that marked the Mordy train stop, as I started to wonder how we were going to get back. We asked the taxi driver to come back for us in a couple of hours, paid him for the fare and negotiated a high fare for the return.

A couple of hundred feet farther, we found the small, rectangular square where Moishe's family's store had been. It was eerie. It seemed that time had stood still.

The square was adorned with a neatly manicured patch of grass, its focal point a military statue. Along either side of the square ran the main road, lined with its original wooden commercial structures. Some were boarded up but others were nicely painted in a variety of colors. The one we counted-off as Moishe's was painted blue. They were no people in the square since we had traveled on a holiday, as we learned, but none of the structures looked abandoned.

Some of the other buildings were more modern but most seemed to be in their original state, watched over by unseen spirits. A one-lane road ended at each of the square's corners. We walked down the dirt and gravel road leading from the northwest corner to small abandoned farms where chicken coops still stood. The buildings seemed to house the ghosts of residents past as well as their chickens. We saw no evidence of electricity or indoor plumbing. When we'd talked to Pesche about her time in Mordy many years earlier, she'd recalled, "A man came with a machine and made electricity. Each family's treasure was a horse or a cow."

We were grateful to see our driver two hours later. At our request, he spoke to a couple of old men, standing on the corner watching our every move, to ask whether they had known the Huber family and whether they knew the whereabouts of the Jewish cemetery. We watched as they shook their heads at the photos he showed them. But, based on their directions, the driver took us down a well-paved, modern road leading from the southeast corner of the square and lined with far-reaching grain fields. Off the road we found the hidden, abandoned old Jewish cemetery.

Trying not to step on any graves, we walked among fallen moss-covered headstones, carved with faded Hebrew lettering and Jewish symbols, disappearing under many layers of decayed vegetation. This place was creepy. In awe of the history lost in this cemetery, we searched in vain for a headstone with a familiar family name and left wishing we could find a way to restore the cemetery.

In Munich, we wanted to find the house where Herm was born. We started our research at the Munich Jewish Museum to see if we could learn any more about life at the DP (Displaced Persons) camp and confirm its former location. The Museum had few records, but we found a map of the neighborhood. It appeared to show that the community had been razed and replaced with an industrial complex.

Having traveled so far, Herm insisted we go anyway to the location, in search of some connection to the place where his parents had lived, where his brother Lenny had played soccer, and he was born. The neighborhood was far from the city center. To get there, we had to go by subway, tram, bus, and foot. Then, suddenly, after we'd walked down a couple of streets, there it was. The maps were wrong! It was like seeing a distant oasis in the desert. We could make out a street sign, "Spitzer Strasse."

We walked through several more local streets until we finally arrived at a nicely maintained communal park with a grassy lawn and playground, sitting at the entrance of the former DP camp. The planned community, we learned, was known as Siedlung Kaltherberge. With great anticipation, we walked quickly down the quiet streets to a house that had the same number Herm remembered from his mother's stories.

While we stood outside, staring, wondering and taking pictures, the homeowner came outside. He was wary we'd been sent by the cable company to investigate illegal tapping into their wires. "No, no, no, we are not with the cable company. I was born in this house," said Herm, so moved that his voice cracked, bringing all of us to tears. The man's attitude changed immediately and Walter and his wife Simone became extremely hospitable and taken with the story. They couldn't do enough for us, and welcomed us like returning family.

Herm and Milo uncovering broken headstones covered in moss in the old Jewish cemetery outside Mordy.

The little house with the picket fence where Herm was born no longer exists. It's been replaced with a new structure built by its current residents in the 1980s, but the community is still there, as are a few of the original homes.

Apparently, no other refugee had ever come back, and many younger members of the community had no idea of the area's history and its vital role immediately after the war. A proud community, it had celebrated its 75th anniversary the year before we arrived. Walter insisted we take home their beautiful beer stein commemorating the community's anniversary as a remembrance of our visit.

Now, the homeowners, who have since become our friends, tell us that Siedlung Kaltherberge is interested in a commemoration of its history, with the cooperation of the Munich Jewish Museum. The elders want to teach younger Germans about the refugees who tried to put their lives back together in their neighborhood before moving on to places with less painful memories.

Until my mother's disclosure, Bucharest's only significance to me was as my birthplace. However, as part of our pilgrimage, we continued to Bucharest in search of the house my parents owned and where they'd lived between 1947 and 1951.

Bucharest has been Romania's capital only since 1881, so many of its public buildings are relatively new. It was modeled after Paris, with wide, tree-lined avenues, stretching from grand traffic circles, and even its own Arc de Triomphe. But its once magnificent structures were crumbling. The beauty of its landscaping, overgrown in some places, remained primarily in numerous public parks.

A few years before our pilgrimage, my mother, always a fighter, insisted that I file a claim for return of the house she and Sandu had owned. Now, with the help of a local agent, we went looking for our home. Numerous telephone calls to the housing authority were needed just to find the street Genadi Petrescu, since renamed Strada Cauzasi, tucked in between newer streets. And there, finally, was number 38. Joy! It was a stucco structure, with an ornate Roman-style cornice under the roofline. The house must have been an imposing structure in 1947. Now, sixty years later, the impressive architectural details were cracked and crumbling just as were those of most of Bucharest's historic buildings. The Roma sitting outside under a porch playing chess gave us the same reception we later received from those in the streets of the old Jewish neighborhood in Galati. They were no happier to see us walking around than we were to see them living in our house!

A search we'd commissioned in connection with the claim revealed that the house had been converted into five separate apartments. Some apartments were still owned by the Romanian government. Others had been sold and were in private hands. In any case, all efforts by families like ours to seek compensation or a return of property have been stymied by corrupt government officials, despite numerous orders by the International Court to make restitution. My lawyer has assured me "I will keep working until the day I die to recover Jewish properties wrongfully taken and now in the hands of the Romanian government." I'm afraid the claim will outlive me and the lawyer.

We made no claim for a small shop my parents had purchased in one of the many single-story buildings in the city's tannery district, built at the city limits no doubt to protect residential areas from the noise, smell, and pollution. The shed-like structures still exist today, now home to other small-scale businesses. I stood transfixed in front of a row of these sheds, trying to picture what it must have been like 60 years earlier. They probably hadn't changed much. But the single story, garage-like spaces stood next to a multi-lane roadway and across from tall, modern apartment buildings.

The train line my mother had mentioned so often took us from Bucharest to Galati, the last stop on the pilgrimage. When we arrived at the train station in her beloved Galati, I was disappointed to see little suggestion of the grandeur I'd pictured. In a barren area downhill from the main roadway the new train station, a product of Romania's entry into the European Union, was no more than an aluminum-covered deck adjacent to several train tracks that snaked out into the distance. The station itself was no more than a few platforms, each with only a row of connected plastic seats, the concrete was broken and the paint was faded; the whole structure sunken into the high grass.

When Herm and I began exploring Galati, we used an older map to try to locate the storefront that was so central to both my father's and my grandfather's lives. I was crestfallen to discover that even the street no longer exists. It had been replaced with Soviet block housing. There were few signs of a former Jewish community. As we stood outside the municipal building, a few curious locals approached us. "May we help you?" the oldest of the group asked in Romanian.

"We are searching for a former shoe store, owned by Carol Marcus that used to be on Strada Tecuci on the corner of General Berthelot— about sixty years ago," I replied in my rusty Romanian.

None of them remembered a shoe store, but a woman offered, "There is an old man in this neighborhood who might know. We'll call him."

A few minutes later, a kindly bald man, his back humped over, shuffled toward us. Again, I explained in Romanian what we were looking for. The elderly man responded, "Please forgive me, my dear one, I don't remember it either," in the formal manner of speech, that had never been familiar to me, since I'd learned to speak at home.

But I was exhilarated to be sharing details of my family's history, standing on the same streets where my parents and grandparents had walked, and talking to a man who must have been there when they were, too.

The locals did direct us to the synagogue, built around the turn of the century. Overflow from a detached gutter damaged parts of the roof but there was evidence that efforts were being made to keep the large Byzantine-style structure in good repair. Next door to the synagogue was a large, three-story brick building that we thought must have been my mother's school.

Around the corner was a narrow residential street, stretching perpendicular to the street where my grandfather's store might have been. We walked up the street as slowly as we dared, taking in the small, dilapidated buildings, now inhabited by squatting Roma. We had been warned that local populations felt threatened by returning Jews making claims for confiscated properties. Squatters sitting in pairs, on low stools outside their doors, warily watched us.

Finally, the friendly locals we'd first met directed us to a Jewish cemetery, being cared for by a middle-aged woman who lived on the grounds. To supplement her meager salary, the caretaker grew her own vegetables, raised chickens and ducks, and even had a goat. She appeared to be living a rather solitary life among the cemetery's ghosts.

My parents' house in Bucharest, the exterior now cracked and crumbling.

A memorial to Jewish lives lost during the First
World War, erected by the Sacred Society of the
Hebrew Community of Galati.

As we approached the tall iron gates, we were greeted by a short,
stocky woman, sporting a huge cross on her blouse and she wore a
long skirt, covered with an apron, both in ill-matched, multi-colored
patterns; her hair was covered with a brightly colored kerchief. "May
we come in and visit the cemetery?" I asked.

"No, it is the Shabbat," she replied. I was quite impressed that
she took her responsibilities so seriously. But we knew that it is not
forbidden by Jewish law or custom to visit a cemetery on Shabbat.

"We would like to make a contribution for the cemetery," I said,
already feeling more comfortable with my improving Romanian. As I
showed her a generous gratuity, her demeanor changed.

"Do you have head coverings?" she asked, holding out a kippah for my husband. She nodded in approval as I put on the scarf I brought for that purpose.

The cemetery was not well maintained; many headstones were overgrown with vegetation. Yet, it was in a quiet spot, on the outskirts of the city, and spring flowers perfumed the air.

As we walked around, we noticed a gnome-like mortician standing at the entranceway to the mortuary building and staring at us with bulging eyes. Sporting a black knit hat and wide peasant pants held up by a rope belt, he arrived to prepare for another funeral. I was surprised that the cemetery is still in use, awaiting the few remaining Jews of Galati.

We wandered the hallowed grounds until we came across a headstone with Mamaia's maiden name of Zisman. Was it a relative? There was no one left to ask.

Chapter Twenty-Four

FAST FORWARD

AT OUR MOST RECENT Passover Seder, there were so many loved ones sitting around our parallel dining room tables, I could not help but reflect on the sacrifices and choices that brought us there. The dining room was brightly lit and the tables were set with Rebecca and Michael's best and only china, best stainless steel silverware, and sparkling new crystal goblets. I felt great satisfaction, sitting peacefully and observing the festivities, now being hosted by our oldest daughter and her husband.

There was Lenny, still fit with a full head of hair (and less gray than Herm's) and his warm-hearted wife Rhea, a newer member of the family. Periodically, I could still hear his voice rise above the others in peals of laughter. Sarita had passed away in her mid-fifties after a short and painful struggle with an aggressive colon cancer. She and I did really love each other. We met when I was 18 and Sarita was 25 and were close before we wasted precious years estranged from each other because of an inappropriate accusation I made during a petty argument about child rearing. For the next 15 years, she would not forgive me. At last, I saw forgiveness in her eyes the last time we met, which was the greatest gift she could have given me. Sarita was survived by two wonderful, beautiful daughters, Lisa and Tami, who were adults, but still young and vulnerable when she passed away.

Near Lenny was Lisa, who married David, her ideal husband, always patient and supportive not to mention loving. During their childhood, my girls always looked up to Lisa, their idol, and fought over who would get the sleeping bag next to her. Our efforts to keep our families close have paid off with memorable family gatherings. Lisa developed into a caring mom to Evan, Sam, and Jordan and a success with her own analytics career, having given up an equally successful side business as a baker.

Her sister, Tami, not to be outdone, has two successful careers. She is employed as a marine biologist for the Smithsonian Institute. She is also a talented singer, appearing with bands in the Annapolis area. Although not present at the Seder because she lives too far to attend, Tami always comes to mind. Herm and I see Tami as often as we can.

Sitting near Lisa, and always seen laughing together at family gatherings are our three daughters with their husbands and their children, our seven grandchildren—namesakes for many of our family members introduced in this memoir. Our oldest daughter, Rebecca, was named after my father, Baruch, aka Sandu. She was born while we lived in married student housing at Rutgers. She spent many an hour sleeping, bent over her scooter-chair at Herm's lab while he was finishing his graduate research. Her husband Michael is the family's marvelous chef in addition to his very successful management information systems career. They are amazing parents to their three children, Sophie, Lila, and Marcus. Rebecca has become a wonderful, very happy, partly stay-at home mom, who uses her education in nutrition and science as a part-time instructor and administrator at Montclair State University. She is a thoughtful and introspective woman who has taken a role as mother hen to her sisters. I believe this was a natural development for her given the number of times I called on her to watch them for me over the years.

Our middle daughter, Rayna, was named after one of Pesche's sisters, Shoshana, who perished in the War. Rayna was born as we were transitioning from college to work with responsibilities for house and children. She was always so gentle and quiet at a time when we needed it. Always a hard worker in school, she went on to become an architect. She and her husband, Esteban, also a creative architect, from Argentina, are very caring and dedicated parents to Milo and Paloma. Esteban is also the family artist, illustrating Herm's children's books and teaching the young ones how to water color "properly," as his niece Pepper reported to her pre-school class. Rayna, Esteban and their children annually spend time in Argentina with Esteban's family. Esteban's mother, Perla, a singer of Yiddish songs and a well-known geologist, has joined us for the Seder this year, bringing homemade gefilte fish based on an old Polish family recipe. Thankfully for her in-laws Perla and Lito, Rayna has a facility with languages and has learned to speak Spanish fluently. Rayna has become the family historian since she arranged our family pilgrimage to Europe.

Sara Marci, our youngest daughter, was named after Mamaia and Moishe. She and her husband, Jeremy, are also creative forces in our family, Jeremy being our grandchildren's entertainer, hence the *interesting* names for their children, Ziggy and Pepper. Sara is the lead user experience web designer for her group at a large insurance company and Jeremy is a talented sports producer and video editor. At every Seder he is also in charge of madcap entertainment for the youngsters. Jeremy can usually be found with Michael, David, and Esteban outside, drinking a beer as they genuinely enjoy one another's company. They might also be throwing around a football for the boys, Evan, Sam, Milo, and even young Marcus, who is not to be denied his place. As a child, Sara was always the comedian, finding ways to make us laugh, and easily making friends. As an adult, she almost always has a smile on her face.

Before the meal, all the children played roles in a grand Passover play worthy of Cecille B. DeMille, written by Herm and in costumes

with props created by him from household items; cotton balls on
a medical mask for a beard, golf balls for hail, and hundreds of tiny
plastic insects for the plagues. Such a funny and raucous Seder! Milo, at
times a bit oppositional, was perfectly cast as Pharaoh. All he had to do
in response to Moses's frequent demands to "Let my people go" was
shout, "No!"

As I looked around the room, I could also imagine those loved ones
who were no longer with us, sitting around the Seder tables, laughing,
talking, singing, as they used to do.

Sadly, Sandu had been the first to die, as I've said earlier, in 1971,
in the second year of our marriage. I'd always lamented that he'd died
before he could meet any of his grandchildren. He would have been
surprised at how much joy they would have brought him.

Moishe was the next to die in 1977 having experienced the
satisfaction of helping us finish the construction of the basement of
our first home and attending Herm's graduation with a doctorate
in psychology from Rutgers University. I'd received my bachelor's
degree at the same ceremony, holding Rebecca and already pregnant
with Rayna. Moishe had experienced great joy from baby Rebecca,
who knew just which strings to pull to get whatever she wanted from
grandpa. She would gently stroke his rough chin at bedtime, pleading,
"No bed. No bed." He always gave in when he and Pesche were
babysitting. Rayna crawled all over him as he lay in a hospital bed in
the weeks before his death.

Pesche died in 1999, age 88 or 89. No one ever really knew
her real birthdate. She had been present for the birth of each of her
grandchildren, and lived to see them called a Bat Mitzvah and graduate
from college. She almost lived long enough to attend Rebecca
and Michael's wedding. After spending more than 20 years in their
Overlook Hills home, she'd lived for a short while at an assisted living
facility, just down City Line Avenue. Tragically, greatly diminished

by Alzheimer's disease, her last days were spent in a nursing home. Together, Lenny and Herm visited her every week and supported one another in their sorrow.

Lily and Lulu divorced after about thirty years of marriage. Lulu's time in the labor camp had left him vulnerable and he turned to his faith more and more as he got older. By the time he passed away, he had given away all his worldly possessions and lived in a single room in Montreal. He continued to visit Lily in Toronto. He also visited my mother since they had both been left to grow old in Montreal. He dedicated his life to prayer and wore the long beard and clothes of the orthodox Jew.

My mother was the last to die in 2012, also age 89. She too suffered from dementia and severe medical problems, and despite my best efforts, I could not ease either her profound psychic or physical misery in the last year of her life. Her passing was undoubtedly a relief for her, and frankly it was a relief for me too. She had seen and survived it all, including another emigration from her beloved Canada to an assisted living facility in New Jersey, where Herm and I visited her often. I refused to let her be alone and forgotten, and she wasn't. Netty was there for all three of her granddaughters' weddings in New Jersey, New York, and Ontario.

We did not think Netty's and her sister Lontzi's last visit together would be their final one. Netty had traveled to Buenos Aires for Rayna's and Esteban's post-nuptial party in 2003 where she met up with Lontzi who had come from San Paulo. But, alas, Lontzi died several years later.

In 2005, Netty, Herm, and I visited with my Aunt Lily, then living in Toronto near her daughter, Anna. We'd all had such a sad visit, knowing this would be the last time they saw each other. Lily had survived Lulu, but died a year after Netty did.

Netty held on as long as her dementia would permit, determined and tenacious, just has she had been fifty years earlier when she insisted we go to Atlantic City. For that I will be ever grateful to her.

Strangely, despite these loved ones missing from the Seder, I was not sad. I felt hopeful and understood the endless cycle that is life. Looking at the loving faces of those around me, and remembering the happy and meaningful moments with those no longer there, centered me.

The family traveled to Montreal for Netty's burial; she'd made me promise it would take place there. Ironically, we stayed with our children and grandchildren in Ruby Foo's across the street from the hotel where Herm and his family had stayed on their first visit, almost fifty years earlier. A year later we attended the unveiling of Netty's footstone, on a gravesite she shared not with Sandu, but with her second husband, Simon Glazer. Netty and Simon, married less than a year after Sandu died, were happy for 20 years. Simon was my stepfather, my third father and a grandfather to our children.

Lenny, who had known Netty for 47 years, presided over the service. It poured the entire weekend.

EPILOGUE

I UNDERSTAND NOW why I could never become Secretary of State as
Madeline Albright did. Unlike the groundbreaking path she chose, I'd
chosen a safe path. My plan was a traditional one. I would get married.
I would work and support Herm while he pursued a doctorate. We
would have a dozen children. Despite my many interests, I never
thought about what would come after marriage and children or what
else there might be for me. Unlike me, Madeline Albright had wide,
unending vision and ambition.

My own vision came from movies and books. Observing the
fictional romantic lives of others, I came to believe in the possibility
of living a fairy tale life. I'd always wanted the fairy tale. And, I got the
fairy tale. I met a handsome, blue-eyed man who whisked me away
from my ordinary, sometimes difficult existence, to a romantic one, far
from family, friends and memories, all the way to another country. It
was a migration much like the one each of our families made, though
not as easily and willingly as I did.

In many other ways, my life has been a fairy tale. So much so that
when I've told others about my life's story, many have suggested I

write a memoir. But it is not my story alone. It is also the story of the people who made profound choices and sacrifices that made my fairy tale come true.

I grew up before the Women's Liberation Movement had become a household word. My ambition to become a lawyer did not take hold until I was in my early twenties, already married with two children. Coming from one immigrant family and marrying into another, I had no blueprint for the modern world. No one had gone to college. No one was a lawyer. No one had aspired to more than making a living and being a good person. It took a long time for me to realize the wonderful role models I had in Mamaia, Netty, and Pesche. They were strong, courageous, and willing to take great risks to protect their families so that their legacy might live on. I found that it was how I lived my life and taught my daughters to live theirs. Is that not, after all, the meaning of life?

Acknowledgments

Many people contributed their time and energy to helping with this five-year effort. I am particularly grateful to my mentor and friend, Barry Blank, English teacher par excellence, who spent the better part of two years thoughtfully and gently guiding my efforts. Essentials of grammar, how to flesh out memories, how to remain on the path, and figuring out what should stay in or not, are valuable skills he taught me.

Much appreciation to my editor Bibi Wein, who performed a behemoth task by arranging and re-arranging, and always insisting that she wanted to know more details. Yet, she somehow always kept sight of the big picture.

Margo Greenfield offered kind support and made me think about what I was really trying to say. I conducted interviews and research about critical themes and events of the 20th century, and I am indebted to Leonard Huber, Samuel Feldmus, Fay Swita, and Murray Goldfinger for their memories.

I also owe a debt of gratitude to the instructors at The Writers Circle who helped me find my memoir voice after 30 years of legal writing, especially Sondra Regine Gash and Vinessa DiSousa. Jim Malcolm, expert on the Oxford comma, and eagle-eyed Mary Zanes, expert at saying "I don't understand what you wrote," were valuable proofreaders. Adept Content Solutions created a professional interior design, helping to make the memoir come to life.

My three girls, Rebecca, Rayna, and Sara, offered warm daughterly support and specific advice that made this a better book. Their profound interest in their mother's story was touching.

Finally, this book would never have seen the light of day without the unrelenting support of my blue-eyed boy, Herm, who would not let me quit and who floated with me down memory lane.

90321921R00113

Made in the USA
Columbia, SC
02 March 2018